lot 5a

The Art of Mariano Azuela:
Modernism in
La malhora, El desquite, La luciérnaga

by
Eliud Martínez

Introduction by Luis Leal

Latin American Literary Review Press

Series: Explorations

Pittsburgh, Pennsylvania, 1980

The Latin American Literary Review publishes Latin American creative writing under the series title *Discoveries,* and critical works under the series title *Explorations.*

© Copyright 1980 by Eliud Martinez.

Library of Congress Cataloging in Publication Data:

Martinez, Eliud, 1935-
    The Art of Mariano Azuela.
    1. Azuela, Mariano, 1873-1952—Criticism and interpretation. I. Title.
PQ7297.A9Z76   863   79-29682
ISBN 0-935480-02-1

The Art of Mariano Azuela: Modernism in La malhora, El desquite, La luciérnaga can be ordered directly from the publisher, Latin American Literary Review Press
P.O. Box 8316, Pittsburgh, Pennsylvania 15218
for $5.95 plus 80 cents postage and handling.

Dedication

This book is dedicated to my father and mother,
Estroberto and María Martínez,
and to the memory of my grandfather,
Eusebio Martínez-Ortiz

Contents

Acknowledgments

Some of the material of this book has been published in somewhat different form: "La visión alcohólica de Dionisio en *La luciérnaga* de Mariano Azuela," in *Revista Universidad de Sonora*, Vol. III, No. 2, 1972; "Mariano Azuela and 'The Height of the Times:' A Study of *La luciérnaga*," in *Latin American Literary Review*, Vol. III, Fall-Winter, 1974-75; and *"La malhora:* From the Novel of the Mexican Revolution to the Modern Novel," in *Latin American Literary Review*, Vol. IV, Spring-Summer 1976. A shorter version of Chapter III, *"El desquite:* A Study of Point of View," is scheduled for publication by *Hispanófila* soon.

In the writing of this book I became indebted, directly and indirectly, to several persons. Professor M. A. Serna-Maytorena directed me to Azuela's modern novels when I was enrolled in his graduate seminar on Spanish American literature at Ohio University, during 1971-72.

To Professor Luis Leal, distinguished literary critic and historian of Mexican and Spanish American letters, I am indebted for his kindness in the writing of the Introduction, and for the personal interest he has always shown in this scholarly investigation at various stages.

Because this book developed out of my dissertation for the Ph.D. in English and Comparative Literature at Ohio University, Athens, I wish to thank the members of my dissertation committee for guidance, critical assistance and support: Professors Wayne Dodd, David Heaton (Director), Dean McWilliams and M. A. Serna-Maytorena. I am also grateful to Professor Rainer Schulte, editor of *Mundus Artium*, who was Chairman of Comparative Literature when I was a graduate student, for professional and personal guidance in structuring a Ph.D. program of study with a concentration in international Modernism in the arts.

I want to thank my friend and colleague, Professor Hugo Rodríguez-Alcala, for taking the time to read the book manuscript and for his good suggestions. I am grateful to Professor Jean Franco for reading the manuscript and her suggestions. I also wish to thank an anonymous reader of the manuscript for his valuable comments and suggestions, which helped me to make some improvements in the language and content of the text.

For reasons too numerous to mention I am most indebted to Donald L. Weismann, University Professor in the Arts at the University of Texas. As a teacher, and as a friend for more than twenty years, beginning when I was an undergraduate student, Weismann has given me unfailing encouragement and support—moral, spiritual and professional. Because he is an historian and critic of art and a practitioner of several of the arts—poetry, painting, novel and film—it is from him that I first began to acquire some understanding of Modernism in the arts. I trust that something of his sympathy and compassion for human beings and of his love for the life of mind and for the arts comes through in this modest work of literary history and criticism.

I want to thank the University of California at Riverside Committee on Research for two intramural research grants which provided me with funds to carry out this investigation. Last of all, I am most deeply grateful to my wife, Elisse, and to my children, Laura and Tanya, for their patience, devotion and understanding during many lengthy periods of time when work took me away from my duties as husband and father.

Eliud Martínez
University of California, Riverside
August 5, 1979

Introduction

Mariano Azuela occupies a prominent place in the development of the Mexican novel during the first half of the twentieth century. His work marks the transition between the naturalistic novel of French origin and the Novel of the Mexican Revolution, which is the first of American origin to cease imitating European forms. For the Novel of the Mexican Revolution to emerge—precisely with Azuela—a social revolution had to erupt first, one that was to destroy the effeminacy of Mexican literati and bring an end to their servile imitation of European forms.

Before the Revolution, Azuela had limited himself to copying the French in *Mala yerba* and other novels, applying naturalistic techniques unsuccessfully to the depiction of Mexican social reality. Or he imitated the Spanish, as in *Sin amor*, an unsuccessful novel that adds nothing to his development as a novelist. In 1915, however, in the field of battle, far from libraries and medical offices, Azuela discovers a new method of narration, a technique that springs from the desire to show the meaningfulness of the historical events which he is witnessing and in which he is participating. With *Los de abajo*, then, is born not only the Novel of the Mexican Revolution, but also the authentically American novel which is conscious of its social mission, proud to give artistic expression to indigenous matters and themes and in the knowledge of being legitimate in its own right, and not a bastard European imitation.

During the years 1915 to 1925 great political and social changes take place in Mexico that do not permit a flowering of letters and the arts, for which flowering social and personal tranquility is essential. It is astonishing, consequently, that Azuela continued to write novels, at the vortex of the cataclysm, even though they brought him no economic benefits nor fame as a writer. About 1923, because of the apparent failure of the novels which he had already published, Azuela makes the brave resolution, as he himself says in picturesque language, to attract the attention of the public by writing according to the latest technique. Whatever may have been the motive, the truth is that by aban-

1

doning the manner of narration of the Novels of the Mexican Revolution and by trying a new method he creates a narrative which places him in advance of his times and paves the way for the experimental novel.

It is these experimental novels, referred to as "hermetic" (*La malhora, El desquite, La luciérnaga*), that the young critic Eliud Martínez examines and analyzes in this book, which adds a new dimension to the already considerable body of Azuela criticism.

Eliud Martínez did well to choose this hermetic, better still, this vangardist period of Azuela's novels for examination. For the Novels of the Mexican Revolution have been examined and re-examined by the critics from diverse perspectives, and the novels of the post-revolutionary period add nothing—with one or another exception—to the development of the Mexican novel. But the experimental novels point the way already to what will be the Spanish American new novel, as Eliud Martínez rightly emphasizes. His book, amply clear-sighted and at the same time well organized, makes the merits of these works stand out, in relation to the development of the novel, not only in Mexico, but also in Spanish America.

It is true that other critics (Monterde, Leal, Ramos, Schulman, Sommers) had already pointed out in passing the technical and experimental traits of these three novels. But it is not until now, with Martínez's book, that for the first time the problem has been made the center of critical attention. For these reasons Martínez's book makes a valuable contribution to the literary criticism not only of Azuela, but of the Spanish American novel of the twentieth century. Consequently, its publication is to be commended.

Luis Leal
Santa Barbara, California

CHAPTER I

The critical neglect of Azuela's modern novels

Mariano Azuela (1873-1952), according to Luis Leal, "is probably Mexico's best known novelist, both inside and outside his country."[1] The publication of Azuela's complete works, *Obras completas de Mariano Azuela*,[2] between 1958 and 1960, contributed to Azuela's still growing reputation. Published in three huge volumes, the *Obras completas* now makes possible a viewing of Azuela's total creative achievement from several perspectives. His more than twenty novels, novelettes, and short stories fall into four periods: (a) early works, (b) the novels of the Mexican Revolution, (c) the experimental or modern novels, and (d) last works. Moreover, he is the author of several biographical and fictional-biographical works, a two volume autobiography, and numerous critical essays which deal with important French, Spanish and Mexican writers of the nineteenth and twentieth centuries. He has also written plays and reworked some of his novels into plays and films. His *Obras completas*, therefore, and the centenary of his birth in 1973, encourage a renewal of interest in Azuela and his works.

Given his reputation, it seems strange that prior to 1925 Azuela was hardly known even in his native Mexico. In that year, a novel which had been published ten years earlier, *Los de abajo* (*The Underdogs*), was "discovered".[3] Of the ten novels which Azuela had written prior to this date, *Los de abajo*, once discovered and brought to the attention of the critics and the public, almost alone catapulted Azuela into international recognition. In following years this novel went through six editions in Spanish. Since then it has been translated into English, French, German, Yugoslavian, Portuguese, Czechoslovakian, Italian, Japanese, Swedish, Russian and Yiddish. In addition to this novel four of his other novels have been translated into English: *Mala yerba* (1909,

Marcela: A Mexican Love Story), *Las moscas,* and *Los caciques* (1918 and 1914, *Two Novels of Mexico: The Flies* and *The Bosses,* respectively), and *Las tribulaciones de una familia decente* (1918, *The Trials of a Respectable Family*).

All of these novels reflect Azuela's main preoccupation with social and political conditions in Mexico, with national and cultural life, particularly as they were affected by the Mexican Revolution. They are in a very large sense, social or sociological novels, and they exhibit a dominant interest in realism and naturalism, and a decided preference for traditional forms of the novel. To date, these and comparable novels account for Azuela's reputation as the creator of the "Novel of the Mexican Revolution."

These novels of the Mexican Revolution are well known by Azuela scholars and established critics of the Mexican novel both inside and outside of Mexico. They have been the subject of a great number of intensive critical studies in books and articles. Indeed, the bibliography on Azuela as the outstanding novelist of the Mexican Revolution is vast.[4] There is, however, one significant aspect of his work, a period in his trajectory as a novelist, that has been undeservedly neglected. During his third period Azuela wrote three experimental or modern novels: in 1923, *La malhora* (*The Evil One*); in 1925, *El desquite* (*Revenge*); and in 1926, *La luciérnaga* (*The Firefly*). The neglect of these three novels, therefore, points to a serious gap in Azuela studies in particular, and also in the study of the modern Mexican novel.

In recent years some critics of the Mexican novel have called attention to this serious gap. In 1952, for example, Francisco Monterde said that this period deserves much more attention than that which only a few critics have given it.[5] In 1959, when Luis Leal was asked by the *Encyclopaedia Britannica* to prepare a brief article on Azuela, he expressed surprise that no book existed which dealt completely with the author of *Los de abajo.*[6] Commenting on the period of Azuela's modern novels, also in 1959, José Rojas Garcidueñas took issue with the study and classification of novels based on thematic and historical considerations alone. He deplored the lack of critical attention given to technique and other formal elements of the novels of the Mexican Revolution. Addressing himself to Azuela scholars in particular, he noted that the bibliography on Azuela was already very large. He felt, however, that the most extensive studies were somewhat panegyric or obliquely bibliographical. Even the most perceptive evaluations, he felt, addressed themselves only to a single novel or to certain particular aspects of the author. "The truth," states Rojas Garcidueñas, "is that there is still no broad and intensive criticism which might balance Azuela's value in his own right and his repercussions on Mexican letters."[7] And in his Preface to the 1968 single volume paperback edition of the three modern novels, Raymundo Ramos reiterated Monterde's concern.[8]

Leal's book, *Mariano Azuela: vida y obra*, has certainly made great strides toward a balanced analysis of intrinsic and extrinsic[9] elements in Azuela's novels. But his excellent examination of Azuela's craftsmanship and of the three experimental novels is far from being exhaustive. There does not exist, to my knowledge, any serious and intensive investigation which examines in detail the innovative techniques and forms of the three modern novels, singly or as a group, nor one which points out their importance within the trajectory of Azuela's novelistic development.

The first aim of this investigation, then, is to critically analyze and interpret each of the three modern novels. Since *La malhora, El desquite,* and *La luciérnaga* are characterized by an unprecedented concern with technical experimentation and other matters of craft, and particularly since they have been undeservedly neglected, it seems appropriate to make the kind of intensively critical analysis of these novels which Rojas Garcidueñas has rightly indicated is presently lacking. In carrying out the first aim of this investigation I have kept in mind Azuela's earlier novels, particularly those of the Mexican Revolution. Because they are so well known, my comments are limited to pointing out features and general characteristics, both thematic and formal, which suggest Azuela's artistic evolution, especially towards Modernism. In dealing with the modern works singly, I have been attentive to evidence that makes apparent Azuela's continuing formal development beyond the novels of the Mexican Revolution.

A second aim of this investigation is to estimate the collective significance of the three modern novels. Collectively the three fictional works make a strong case for the need to recognize Mariano Azuela's much larger artistic achievement than is now appreciated. Such a case is strengthened when one becomes aware of the heavy emphasis which Azuela critics have placed on extrinsic elements of his works. The evidence of unprecedented technical experimentation in the three modern novels lends still additional weight to the need for re-evaluating Azuela's art.

As I show in this investigation, the critical neglect of Azuela's modernism has perpetuated, until now, an incomplete critical estimate of his art. To make it more complete it was necessary for me to deal with two very important, related factors. One is Azuela's theoretical conception of the novel, with which I deal throughout this investigation. My investigation discusses the influence of Balzac, Zola and others on Azuela's art and on his conception of the novel. The most useful document for understanding this novelistic conception and his literary principles is his autobiographical *El novelista y su ambiente*. Writing in retrospect of the genesis of his fictional works and of his craft Azuela provides his readers with a running commentary that may be compared in many respects and in importance to Henry James' Prefaces to his own novels. It is a known fact that James' Prefaces were also written retrospectively, between 1907 and 1909. The second factor concerns the impact of European and North American avant-garde tendencies on Azuela's three modern works. Indeed, there exists no study, to my knowledge, of such an impact on Azuela's fiction of the twenties.

To deal with the impact of modern European and North American artistic and intellectual tendencies I have employed José Ortega y Gasset's idea of "La altura de los tiempos" ("the height of the times"), an idea which he formulated and developed in one of his most famous books: *La rebelión de las masas* (*The Revolt of the Masses*).[10] "The height of the times," according to Ortega, refers to the vitality of the times, that is, to the intellectual and spiritual potentialities which prevail during any given historical period. He observes that different historical periods exhibit and generate higher or lower levels of creative and spiritual plenitude. In a given age, he maintains, an individual feels with greater or lesser clarity his own relation to his age; he can feel

6

himself to be ahead of or behind the times. For the man of traditional bent, Ortega maintains, the modern age produces anguish:

> The speedy *tempo* which today marks the march of things, the impetus and energy with which everything is done, anguish the man of traditional bent, and this anguish reflects the imbalance between his pulse and the pulse of the age.[11]

The feeling of this imbalance, for Ortega, is inherent in the use of the word *modern*. He says that the word *modern* expresses a consciousness of a new life which surpasses the past. At the same time, he adds, it expresses an imperative to be at the height of the times. "For modern man not to be *modern* is equivalent to falling below the historical level."[12]

Ortega's idea provided me with a basis to suggest that Azuela's venture into the use of modern European narrative forms and techniques was dictated by historical and artistic imperatives of the times during which he wrote the experimental fiction. In the conclusions of this investigation I suggest, moreover, that the idea of the height of the times also applies to the novels of the Mexican Revolution. Traditional and modern alike, Azuela's novels are works of art and social documents which reflect the novelist's deeply personal and artistic response to his times.

In developing his idea Ortega y Gasset does not speak of art, but the idea is clearly transferable to the arts. In examining his relation to the modern age, Azuela, a man of traditional bent, felt himself to be behind the times, below the level of its artistic plenitude. For indeed during the years immediately preceding the period of his modern novels the age was charged with a vigorous intellectual and artistic energy; Modernism became an international fact. To be modern became an imperative.

In Mexico, Azuela felt this imperative; he aspired to be and became modern, but he was anguished by the feeling that he had succumbed to the modern spirit, as he poignantly admitted (III, 597-98). Azuela's ambivalent attitude to modernism, how it clashes with his own theoretical conception of the novel, has adversely influenced his critics' estimates and neglect of the modern

7

novels. It has limited, I believe, the appreciation of his art. For this reason his scorn of the modern receives close examination in this investigation.

In my technical analyses of *La malhora, El desquite* and *La luciérnaga* I have allowed myself to be guided by the works themselves. I have identified those aspects of the novels which are inescapably dominant and which stamp these three works as modern. Admittedly Modernism is a multifaceted artistic phenomenon, and numerous respectable definitions of Modernism have been advanced by countless able literary critics. There is considerable disagreement, however, about Modernism, and some critics even proclaim its demise in order to promote the concept of Postmodernism.[13] Nevertheless, considerable critical agreement about Modernism makes it a manageable concept and framework for an investigation of this kind.

Given this agreement, the fascinating debate concerning the death of Modernism falls outside the scope of the present investigation. Here, I have stressed extremely well known aspects of the modern novel. Modern novels, for example, exhibit a striking and continuous experimentation with forms and techniques. This trait reflects, moreover, the modern novelist's rejection of external standards of reality and a decided preference for depicting the interior reality of fictional characters. The modern novelist is concerned with "the atmosphere of the mind," with fictional renderings of the way that the mind works. As a consequence of its "inward turning," the modern novel also exhibits other traits which distinguish it from the conventional or traditional novel. Characters are uncommonly introspective. They usually have to cope with inner obsessions and problems, with fantasies and memories, and with hallucinations and nightmares. So that depictions may successfully render characters' states of consciousness the modern novelist handles time structurally, in a way that seems fragmented, confused and chaotic. Narrative development is, for this reason, discontinuous. The modern novelist avoids the employment of linear, chronological time. He prefers, rather, psychological time, and he employs the complex narrative methods of point of view and stream of consciousness. These, then, are generally accepted aspects of the modern novel which are dominant in *La malhora, El desquite* and *La luciérnaga.* It is on them and on other narrative elements that this investigation focuses.

In closely examining and analyzing aspects of Modernism in Azuela's experimental fiction I was led to emphasize the chronological trajectory of his art. To show how Azuela arrived ultimately at the stream of consciousness novel my investigation makes an intensive critical analysis and an interpretation of each of the three experimental works, singly and in chronological order. Chapter II seeks to demonstrate that *La malhora* reflects Azuela's continuing adherence to naturalistic principles and narrative methods. It also shows that this novel marks a significant literary advance towards Modernism. Chapter III closely examines two literary advances in *El desquite:* the use of a "dramatized narrator" or a "narrator-agent"[14] to provide the main focus of narration for this second novel, and the narrative method of point of view. Chapter IV deals with *La luciérnaga* as a novel of visions. In this chapter I am concerned with demonstrating that Azuela mastered the narrative methods of point of view and stream of consciousness, and numerous structural forms and techniques of the modern international novel, many of which he had experimented with in the two previous works. So that the reader who is unfamiliar with Spanish may judge the accuracy of my assertions and interpretations I have translated generously many passages from the three works.

Since secondary sources dealing with Azuela's modern novels are almost non-existent, the analyses and interpretations of these works are my own. But my investigation is based, nevertheless, on what may be considered a reasonable familiarity with the main secondary sources that deal specifically with Azuela's novels of the Mexican Revolution and generally with international Modernism in the arts.

Chapter V draws conclusions about the collective significance of the three modern novels and re-appraises Azuela's art. Here, the literary traits of the three works are clearly and systematically summarized, and these predicate the criteria for judging the works' intrinsic and extrinsic values. These criteria, ranked in order of importance, are formal, social, historical and biographical. Formal analysis makes it possible to demonstrate that Azuela significantly enlarged his creative literary resources, that through experimentation he became competent in the handling of complex narrative methods and techniques, some of which reflect the modern cross-fertilization of the arts. His modern works combine elements of naturalism and Modernism. Hence his works continue to have value as social commentary. A survey of critical estimates throughout my investigation, moreover, points out the historical importance of Azuela and his work, an importance which the present investigation enlarges. His place in literary history, in addition, is clarified by locating his works nationally and internationally, within the "spirit of the age," and within the context of international literary influences. Emerging avant-garde artistic and intellectual developments are identified and given some attention.

In Azuela's writing, then, social, historical and formal values converge. He is Mexican and international, and the creator of the Novel of the Mexican Revolution as well as of the modern Mexican novel of consciousness. When considered in light of the novelist's traditional theories of fiction the biographical value of the modern works can be appreciated. Writing the experimental fiction caused deep personal anguish for Azuela, and this distress cannot be underestimated when one considers that the author himself never came to terms with his own modernism. Finally, Chapter V demonstrates that Azuela's three works challenge present critical views that the modern Mexican novel begins with José Revueltas' *El luto humano* (1943) or with Agustín Yanez's *Al filo del agua* (1947, *At the Edge of The Storm*).[15] And the challenge is based on the literary traits and values of *La malhora, El desquite* and *La luciérnaga,* and on the re-appraisal which they authorize. This re-appraisal will begin with a detailed analysis of *La malhora.*

CHAPTER II

La malhora:
from the novel of
the Mexican Revolution
to the modern novel

La malhora (*The Evil One*) of 1923, Azuela's tenth novel, comes five years after *Las moscas* (*The Flies*) and *Las tribulaciones de una familia decente* (*The Trials of a Respectable Family*), one year after the beginning of the great Mexican mural painting movement and two years before the discovery of *Los de abajo* (*The Underdogs*), which establishes Azuela as *the* novelist of the Mexican Revolution. By this time the modern spirit sweeping through Europe had generated a tremendous intellectual and artistic energy which brought winds of change to North America and Mexico. Such European artistic tendencies as cubism, futurism, dada, surrealism and other manifestations of the modern spirit in the arts, and the esthetic ideas behind them, crossed the Atlantic. Avant-garde tendencies, particularly post-modernismo and *estridentismo*, attest to their presence in Mexico. The contemporáneos, while not yet so called, were already engaged in numerous creative activities which dealt with new international esthetic ideas and literary problems.[1] Their activities were marked by cosmopolitan attitudes and by a rejection of prevailing Mexicanismo attitudes. It is in this context that Azuela composed *La malhora*.

During those five years following the last novels of the Mexican Revolution, Azuela pondered the new forms and narrative techniques gaining currency as the modern novel continued to evolve internationally. He was distressed by his anonymity and by the critical neglect of his nine previously published novels. Measuring his own pulse against that of the height of the times he felt an imbalance; and years later, in his autobiography, *El nove-*

11

lista y su ambiente (*The Novelist and His Times*), he clearly documents this distress and the compelling force of the height of the times: to be modern, to evolve. Commenting in that autobiography, in 1951, Azuela said:

> Tired of being an author known only in my own home, I made the brave resolution to attract the attention of the public by writing according to the latest technique. I studied that technique carefully and came to the conclusion that it consists simply in the use of the well-known trick of distorting words and phrases, of deliberately making concepts and expressions obscure to obtain the effect of novelty.[2]

This statement is revealing, first of all because "Azuela was abreast of developments in the European novel; he was familiar with the most recent innovations in the genre arriving from France, England and the United States; and he was also up to date on the criticism of the novel."[3] The statement also reveals his attitude towards the modern novel and his predilections for naturalism, on which he had been weaned. Indeed, in 1938, Azuela had acknowledged the outstanding influences on his writing. On his early novels, he recognized Balzac, Zola, Flaubert, the Goncourts, and Daudet as influences; on the novels of the Mexican Revolution, he acknowledges no identifiable influences; and on his experimental novels, he names Conrad and Proust as influences. He felt, however, that Proust could not have influenced his writing because he was "unique and inimitable" (III, 1280).

In 1947, twenty-five years after the publication of *Ulysses*, Azuela stated that he had read twice the complete works of Marcel Proust. But, he added, "in thirty years I have been unable to finish *Ulysses* by James Joyce" (III, 569). The five year exaggeration seems to speak for itself; this exaggeration could also mean that Azuela had tried to read *Ulysses* soon after its publication in 1922.

Azuela's less than respectful attitude towards the forms and techniques of the modern European novel is also patent in other statements. The technique of the modern novel, he wrote, was a "well-known trick," its methods are "foolish" and soon pass out of fashion (III, 1114). Azuela deplored "certain pretentious and foolish little works, infected by (con pujos de) existentialism, surrealism and other fashionable isms." In reality, he stated, such works "are only awkward imitations of decadent European literature" (III, 1100-21). About the reading public's neglect of his works and of his novelistic practice, Azuela says:

> This [neglect] hurts me more than the applause of the literati would make me happy. . . . I am and have always admitted it, a popular novelist, and what I write is for the people and not for the literati, for which reason what interests me most is to write a book that will be as widely read as possible (III, 1118).

Yet, by 1951, Azuela felt compelled to acknowledge the necessity for a novelist to evolve and to modify and renew his artistic forms. But he holds tenaciously to the notion of the modern novel as trickery. In his autobiography, he adds:

> I am aware too that in the novel the trick is as important as in palm-reading. . . . Both the novelist and the palm-reader address the public which is fickle, capricious and demanding. . . . The novelist lives with the constant threat that . . . his books will remain . . . in the bookseller's warehouses and that the bookseller will close his doors to him if the novelist does not develop new narrative methods and forms (III, 1118).

Azuela's anguish is even more poignantly expressed in the following statement, also from his autobiography:

> I was never stimulated by success and failure has always goaded me on. To overcome the obstacles in my path has been perhaps one of my greatest pleasures, and criticism which is biased and unfair over-

joys me and makes me laugh with unusual euphoria
(III, 1117).

Such statements convey Azuela's life-long and ambivalent attitude towards modernism. He correctly recognized the necessity of experimenting with and developing new narrative forms. But he seems not to have recognized at the time he began to write his modern novels that the "new technique" entailed a much more complex set of principles than he realized, which he felt compelled to observe, and did observe with reluctance and with subsequent regrets. These new principles increasingly inform the structure and techniques of his three modern novels as Azuela evolves from *La malhora* and *El desquite* to *La luciérnaga*. All three of these works, therefore, must be understood as having been generated by the imperative of the height of the times: to be modern.

To write the modern novels, Azuela says in *El novelista y su ambiente*, he abandoned his usual manner of composition. This usual manner of composition, he explains, "consisted in expressing myself, as far as my abilities permitted, with clarity and conciseness" (III, 1114). *La malhora*, then, does in fact represent a significant but a partial change in Azuela's usual narrative methods. This change is characterized by Azuela's increased consciousness of craft, by his preoccupation with the interior lives of the novel's characters, and by experimentation with novelistic structure and technique.

But the work itself holds forth considerable evidence of Azuela's loyalty and adherence to several novelistic principles of the naturalistic or social novel, as he had observed them in the novels of the Mexican Revolution. Azuela's indebtedness to his French masters, Balzac, Zola and the Goncourts, is especially obvious in *La malhora*'s subject matter, characterization, setting, method and in some of its narrative techniques.

As in the novels of the Mexican Revolution, Azuela is directly concerned, like his French masters, with the world around him, with contemporary problems and with social life in particular. Like Balzac, Azuela was of and for the people, a painter of their customs and life. Azuela's subject matter, characters, and setting

14

are based on first-hand experience and direct observation. Like Flaubert and Balzac, Azuela frequently declared that he was concerned with "truth." *La malhora,* moreover, exhibits a number of resemblances to the Goncourt brothers' *Germinie Lacerteux. La malhora* is Altagracia, who is fifteen years old and already a prostitute at the beginning of the novel. Germinie, in the French novel, is fourteen when she comes to Paris. Altagracia is seduced, Germinie is assaulted; and both end up having numerous lovers and succumbing to alcoholism.

There are other resemblances. What is important, however, is the principle of truth, or fidelity to social realities, that is shared by the French and the Mexican novelists. The Goncourt brothers, for example, stated in their preface to *Germinie Lacerteux:*

> We must beg the public's pardon for offering it this book, and give warning of what will be found therein.
>
> The public likes untrue novels: this novel is a true one.
>
> The public likes stories which appear to take place in society: this story comes from the streets.[4]

This statement applies suitably to *La malhora,* for Azuela's novel is also based on literal, documentary truth, and it too comes from the streets. Like *Germinie Lacerteux, La malhora* also deals with the lower classes, with a society below society. Azuela, in addition, like the Goncourts, seems to question whether any social classes are too unworthy, whether any sufferings are too low or whether any tragedies are too foul-mouthed for novelists or readers.[5]

Azuela himself has commented generously on the direct observation and experience on which he drew for the writing of *La malhora.* When he was living and practicing medicine in a slum area of Mexico City, he says in *El novelista y su ambiente,* the material for the writing of *La malhora* was never so abundant and within reach of his hand. But from childhood to adolescence he had met a great variety of shady characters. Consequently he had learned their vocabulary, their gestures, their mannerisms, their slang (caló). His revolutionary wanderings and experiences later enlarged this knowledge, he adds, and when he became a physician treating venereal diseases at a Public Welfare Clinic, situated in the very bowels of Tepito, "there was nothing left for me to learn" (III, 1114).

El Tepito is a slum area in a neighborhood called La Bolsa. During those years, he goes on to say, his patients were inhabitants of that squalid area, the heart and soul of the metropolitan underworld. It was quite common, he continues, to come across men and women sprawled out on the sidewalk, placidly sleeping off their drunkenness in the early morning hours, caressed by the warm bright sun. Azuela reports that he witnessed fights in the street between powerful women who, after hurling at each other the most vile invectives, would grab at each other's tangled hair, exchange blows, sink their teeth into each other until they were bloody and rolling on the ground, driving fists into each other's face. "With elements of this sort," he says, "I composed *La malhora*" (III, 1115).

Azuela closes the third part of *La malhora* with one such street fight between Altagracia and an unnamed woman. The fictional version, however, is even more violent: Altagracia emerges victorious after biting off the earlobe of her opponent who lets out a scream like a rat caught by a trap (II, 970). An ambiguously rendered dog fight opens the part of *La malhora* which follows immediately and considerably dramatizes the women's animal violence. The street fight that Azuela reports and its fictional depiction in *La malhora*, moreover, will remind some readers of the fight in the washhouse, between Gervaise and Virginie, in the first chapter of Zola's *Assommoir*. Zola's novel, it seems safe to say, probably confirmed in Azuela his own feelings that such an incident was suitable subject matter for his novel.

The naturalism of *La malhora*, therefore, is generously in evidence: its method of direct observation and documentation, its characters from the lower classes, and the violence and sordidness of its subject matter. *La malhora* is also a social novel of the city. The setting of the first and fifth parts of the novel is the squalid slums of El Tepito in Mexico City. In *La malhora*, and to a greater extent in *La luciérnaga*, Azuela has depicted his own version of the bowels of a modern metropolitan city, as Zola had done in *Le ventre de Paris*. Again, like his master Zola, Azuela dealt in these two novels with the sordid life of the modern city: alcoholism, prostitution, violence, drugs and murder. Azuela drew his characters from Mexico City's shady underworld: Altagracia; el Flaco and Marcelo, both house painters; and la Tapatía (the name means person from the state of Jalisco in Mexico), the proprietress of the pulquería or pulque tavern El Vacilón.

Azuela's *La malhora* is reminiscent of his first novel, *María Luisa*, which also dealt with the seduction and subsequent degeneration of a young girl. She ends up as a cadaver on the dissecting table of a hospital where her seducer is serving his internship. The "fallen woman" and the prostitute appear frequently in the novels of the Mexican Revolution. Many of these denizens of the underworld reappear under different names in *La luciérnaga*, in a manner reminiscent of Balzac. These traits of *La malhora* emphasize the continuity and consistency of Azuela's art, and underline the persistence of naturalistic principles in his work.

Other characters in *La malhora* make clear the continuity in Azuela's development as a novelist. The prudish and devout Gutierrez sisters and their emphysematous mother remind one of Azuela's characters from respectable middle class families. Such characters appear in several novels of the Mexican Revolution, such as the Viña family of *Los caciques* (*The Bosses*), the Lara-Tellez of *Las moscas* (*The Flies*), and The Vasquez-Prado of *Las tribulaciones de una familia decente* (*The Trials of a Respectable Family*). These families also foreshadow Dionisio's family in *La luciérnaga*. The Porfirista general also is one of Azuela's favorite stock characters. All of them link Azuela's modern novels with the preceding novels of the Mexican Revolution and with the next two modern novels.

La malhora, furthermore, obeys some of Zola's naturalistic principles, spelled out in *The Experimental Novel* of 1880. It also follows Hippolyte Taine's theories concerning the role of heredity and environment in human life. In *El novelista y su ambiente* Azuela states that *La malhora* deals with the case of a girl raised in the sewers.

17

> Her tragedy is the rude tragedy of those creatures
> born in garbage who wane and die with the first rays
> of sunlight; it deals with Altagracia, . . . born with
> many inherited physical and mental flaws, nurtured
> by the ways and morals of the metropolitan under-
> world. Brutally violated by one of them when she is
> just arriving at womanhood she ends up losing the
> rest of what balance remains to her. Under an op-
> pressive obsession for revenge she makes a life for
> herself aimed at killing the abominable man who
> violently broke from the bush the barely budding
> flower (III, 1115).

As mentioned above, at the beginning of *La malhora* Altagracia is barely fifteen years old. In the first of the five parts of the
novel, "Bajo la onda fría" ("During the Cold Spell"), most of the
action takes place inside the pulquería called El Vacilón. Some of
it takes place in the darkened streets of El Tepito, and in a large
hospital room. The first part closes with the discovery of Altagracia's naked and nearly frozen body in the snowy grass of a park on
the Avenida del Trabajo.

In this first part a third person narrator provides the reader
with present and background information on Altagracia; some of
it is placed in the mouth of other characters. The relationships of
the shady underworld characters with each other and with Altagracia are also established. The reader learns that Altagracia's father was murdered by Marcelo, that he is involved with la Tapatía, and that he is the man who seduced Altagracia and pushed her
further on the road toward physical and spiritual degeneration.
Inside El Vacilón, Altagracia dances drunkenly and obscenely on
top of one of the tables. In her tattered and filthy rags, premature-
ly aged, disfigured by dissipation, she already bears the marks of
the victim of squalid surroundings. The third person omniscient
narrator, in a moving passage of the novel, sums up and comments on the effects of environment:

> Shabby disgraceful ballerina, issue of the squalor of
> Tepito, who from Marcelo's arms had passed to

18

countless others and rolled among the gutters and who now on table tops no longer drew even a despicable smile for her obscenities, dragging herself down, lower, she had turned herself into a thing, a thing of the pulquerías, an offensive thing to be resigned or accustomed to (II, 954).

For Marcelo had only pushed Altagracia, offspring of two alcoholics, along on a path she was already travelling. Altagracia's life had been determined by heredity first of all; the first pulque had entered her blood when she was in her mother's womb. Her surroundings compounded those beginnings. This point is given emphasis early in the novel. After identifying the murder victim as her father, Altagracia collapses unconscious. When she revives, she is in a large hospital room. One of the two men investigating the homicide, described by Azuela as a pompous young peacock, interrupts his partner when he asks Altagracia directly if she had known the murder victim; he says:

> —No sir, first the background. Because, don't you know there is no tragedy without cause.
> Alright then, let's proceed in order. First, the stench of a slimy underground (zótano), black as coal smoke, where she was or might have been born, the arches of a large neighborhood in Peralvillo. Secondly, her mother and father passing the days in drunken stupor, and quarreling, until the mother's swollen belly bursts forth with its dark—glorious agave plant! Then the streets, the raunchy cantinas, the slum districts, the stage of Tepito and everything else. The company from which one learns about things; but what things!
> —Perfectly! Don't you see? ... Heredity, upbringing, surroundings. All we need are the causes. In history, in letters, in life, all tragedies have their causes. Don't you know? (II, 958).

19

In the fifth part, also titled "La malhora," almost at the end of the novel, Azuela provides a running summary of Altagracia's life. This summary is given by Altagracia herself in the first person. It too includes an acknowledgement of the influence of surroundings and heredity in her life. The summary from which the following passage is taken is more than two long pages. Altagracia, in half-dialogue, is speaking to a doctor who had been treating her. It seems obvious that he had probed deeply into her sordid past.

> Goodbye, doctor, goodbye! I am leaving, crying over my illness without cure and over the hopes which I leave buried here. . . . I know where I was born and among what people I grew up. It's also true that I don't know how to express myself like decent people, that I'm dumb, but that tone of voice, "what hurts you?" Precisely that hurts me, that nothing should. But this is my skirt of four months ago and this is not my waist of four months ago.
> . . . Oh! If only you like the others had not asked me so much! Because your questions dug up dirt from the bottom of my heart. How many men have I had? Which one did I love the most? Which one do I remember still? Did we do this or that, did we not do . . . ? If after doing with me the rooster flew the coop? . . . And do I long for him and cry over him or dream of him still? Things and things, but I cannot see that they have anything to do with my illness.

In the continuation of her stirring lament, Altagracia provides a clue perhaps to the method Azuela the physician may have used to obtain stories for Azuela the novelist. Altagracia is upset because the doctor will not listen to her account of the symptoms of her illness. She continues:

> Because look at how I try to tell you and tell you what my body feels and you go on, question after question about—begging your pardon, sir—what is

20

my own business. And tell me, doctor, is it just curiosity? Or are you studying to be a lawyer also? . . .

As I leave I am saddened by what you told me yesterday. "Altagracia, you're not even to smell pulque. The world will close up to you all but two paths, the insane asylum or prison." . . . Look, doctor! I was born with pulque in my mouth. Pulque was my blood, my body, and God forgive me, it was my soul (II, 974-75).

In the remaining part of the summary of her life (II, 975-76), Altagracia tells her listener about her seduction and subsequent degeneration. This background information was made known to the reader, by the omniscient narrator at the beginning of the novel, and there are references to it in other parts. The first-person summary, then, refers back to the novel's beginning, which gives it a circular form; the novel ends where it begins, even though it is only in Altagracia's story that there is a going back to the seduction. The seduction must be understood as a significant frame of reference which marks a kind of harsh rite of initiation for Altagracia into other aspects of the squalid life into which she was born.

The divisions of the novel allow for another interpretation. Altagracia's account recapitulates the novel's main episodes beginning with her succumbing to alcohol and marihuana after the seduction. The reader follows, in her own words, the account of her misfortunes and experiences as a servant in the homes; first of the benevolent, insane doctor, then of the prudish and devout Gutierrez sisters, and after that of the old Porfirista general. The account, finally, speaks of her return to the streets and pulquerías.

In the divisions of the novel, retraced by Altagracia's story, Luis Leal sees an innovational quadriform structure, organized around Altagracia, the central character, who never abandons any of the scenes: "The author has structured four episodes, trivial to be sure, in the life of a prostitute and created a new form in the Mexican novel."[6]

The preceding commentary is intended to show Azuela's naturalistic preoccupation with the story of Altagracia's downfall and its causes, heredity and surroundings.

Even more significant is the added structural importance of Azuela's literary strategy of recapitulation which he discovers in *La malhora*. This allows Azuela to give retrospective coherence and continuity at the end of the novel to its fragmented structure, in a way which emphasizes the viewpoint of the central character. For this reason, *La malhora* foreshadows *El desquite* and *La luciérnaga*.

Concerning the novel's naturalism, moreover, *La malhora*, in form and technique, evolves quite naturally out of Azuela's novels of the Mexican Revolution. The episodic and fragmentary structure, which is fundamentally chronological, is carried over from *Los caciques* (*The Bosses*), *Los de abajo* (*The Underdogs*), and *Las moscas* (*The Flies*). Other techniques are also retained from these and other earlier novels: straight conventional narration and exposition, summary, foreshadowing, description, block characterization, author commentary, first person narration, and increased use of dialogue. The characters' points of view, however, begin to take on an enlarged importance.

As one can see, realistic and naturalistic elements are numerous in *La malhora*. In this respect there is, therefore, no really sharp break between the earlier social and the modern novels. Given many of these fictional traits, and given the naturalistic preoccupations of Azuela which they reflect, there can be no denial that *La malhora* is a social novel.[7]

While it is true that *La malhora* is a social novel, it also exhibits Azuela's preoccupation with the consciousness of its two main characters. This preoccupation with interior reality moves Azuela forward toward Modernism.

What is new in *La malhora*, then, is Azuela's use of characters who are plagued by alcoholism and madness: Altagracia and the demented doctor, respectively, and the techniques that Azuela found necessary for depicting their interior lives and states of consciousness. Azuela was therefore compelled, in order to provide a plausible depiction of alcoholic and pathological visions, to experiment with what he called the "new technique." He had to "dramatize"[8] the consciousness of his characters.

Azuela, it is true, had already depicted an alcoholic perception of things in *Las moscas* (*The Flies*). In that novel, following a round of heavy drinking, one of the characters, Donaciano Ríos, remains drunk and half awake after many of the others in the same train car on which he is travelling have passed out. Here are parts of Azuela's depiction, from the beginning of Chapter III, of what Señor Ríos sees and feels:

> Songs ended in hoarse shouts and insane laughter . . .
> Toward midnight they began to give out. Their
> speech became incoherent and inarticulate and then
> hiccoughs, and the weak whimpers that herald the
> approach of insensibility. They lay, legs outspread,
> in a heap of bodies overcome by fatigue and alcohol.[9]

In what follows, as the saying goes, Azuela the author is everywhere. Having set the scene, he then goes on to *tell* the reader about the drunkenness of Donaciano Ríos. Azuela tells the reader what is going on in his mind:

> Señor Ríos could not close his eyes because he had a
> conviction that they were about to be attacked. His
> gaze was fixed on a dark alley. A sudden panic took
> him by the throat. He thought he saw suspicious
> shapes along the right of way. *Good God! The Car-
> ranzistas!* He tried to scream, but his voice failed
> him. *What was the use anyway! The soldiers were
> all dead drunk.* Finally, plucking courage from his
> very agony, he asked himself whether he might be
> the victim of an illusion. . . . He rubbed his eyes and
> explored the landscape more attentively.[10]

The omniscient narrator goes on to tell us what Señor Ríos imagines out there in the darkness as the train pounds along: human figures, Carranzistas attacking, rifle shots. The reader is told that his imagined figures are really telegraph poles. There is a flashback: Señor Ríos imagines himself in his comfortable and peaceful home. Then he passes out and "he dreamed that his escape to the capital on a cattle train was only a dreadful nightmare."[11]

23

With the possible exception of the italicized passages above (not emphasized in the novel) the reader is not really installed in the consciousness of Señor Ríos; his thoughts are not really *shown*.

This kind of conventional narration and exposition carries over into *La malhora*, but Azuela's technique becomes increasingly fragmentary, less discursive, more enumerative and ambiguous. In two sections of the novel, which precede and follow Altagracia's first person account of her downfall, Azuela clearly explores the interior life of Altagracia. At the same time he makes her alcoholic vision serve his lingering concern for exposition and summary.

After Altagracia leaves the doctor to whom she has told her story, she finds the nearest pulquería and she consumes several drinks. The following passage represents Azuela's rendering of the alcoholic frame of mind of Altagracia after these drinks:

> Explosion of images, desires, recollections. Disconnected, absurd, diverse ideas rise and fall in her brain. Multicolored clamor; handclapping and whistles and the daybreak sounds from a non-existent canvas tent; the stupid croaking of a lottery vendor who may not even believe in the peace of the dead; the sorrowful laments of sticky hand organs, the little horses which don't move and the trumpets no one hears. White beds also, and white uniforms and great white halls and tormented silhouettes. The cadaverous countenance of the surgeon and the contradictory gleam of his eyes and his eternally smiling mouth; the hateful and inpenetrable face of an impertinent and prying medical practitioner, the tack-tack-tack-tack of a Singer [sewing machine] and the intolerable murmuring of prayers of three cockroaches who never tire of making the sign of the cross: a rusty crucifix. . . . Overflow of shapeless ideas and feelings, images which fuse and disperse; smash-ups of found longings, sack of insane scorpions (II, 977).

In this passage there seems to be a noticeable effort to efface the omniscient narrator. But Azuela's irony and sarcasm are unmistakable. Exposition here gives way to a piling up of details. There is a marked absence of complete sentences.

The series of flashbacks in this passage provide another, an alcoholic rapid-fire summary of Altagracia's life. The suggestion does not seem implausible that Altagracia, having just reported numerous sordid details from her life to the inquisitive physician, would be still upset, quite naturally, about her misfortunes in life, and be thinking obsessively about them. This passage has the cinematic quality of a rapidly-cut series of short shots in a film that rearranges familiar images, and that uses unusual angles, dramatic lighting effects, close-ups and bizarre imagery to heighten or distort those familiar images and also, depictions of reality or of a character's perceptions of reality. Consequently, the reader is to understand that the above passage reflects thoughts and feelings and images that pass through Altagracia's drunken mind. Altagracia's own awareness of drunken disconnectedness in her thinking, and a sense of how she drunkenly perceives the squalid streets of Mexico City, her stays in hospitals and her employers, the prudish Gutierrez sisters—all this Azuela conveys here with sound modern craftsmanship. The whole passage successfully conveys such symptoms of alcoholism as obsession; an intensification of sensory awareness, visual, auditory, tactile, and olfactory; perturbation; and fantasy. Many parts of *La malhora* taken together exemplify Azuela's use of the techniques of repetition and summary, and they are fundamentally chronological.

Some of the imagery of *La malhora,* as in the passage just given, is surrealistic, as Luis Leal has rightly pointed out:[12] "multicolored clamor," "a nonexistent canvas tent," "the stupid croaking of a lottery vendor," "the little horses which don't move and the trumpets no one hears," "the cadaverous countenance," etc. Many of these characteristics align *La malhora* with the Mexican movement called *estridentismo.*[13]

In all of these ways Azuela, using modern techniques, successfully depicts interior states of Altagracia's mind, assaulted by painful memories and obsessions. In *La malhora,* then, Azuela comes very close to the stream of consciousness method of narration. Azuela's irony and sarcasm intrude however. This intrusion lessens Azuela's success in rendering a sense of the character's simulated flow of thought, that characterizes stream of consciousness. In addition, as I have stated, these approximations to stream of consciousness are too few in number to permit an assertion that Azuela in this novel mastered stream of consciousness. Neither Altagracia's alcoholic vision nor the demented doctor's pathological vision, then, can be said to exhibit Azuela's command of the stream of consciousness method. It is not until *La luciérnaga* that Azuela masters this method.

La malhora does share with stream of consciousness fiction the preference for the interior worlds of the characters and a preoccupation with technique. An examination of the second part of this novel, bearing in mind what has already been said of Altagracia's alcoholic vision, will show this preference and this preoccupation.

The second part of the novel presents the pathological vision of the insane doctor. This part is called "La reencarnación de Lenin" ("The Reincarnation of Lenin"). One important critic of Mexican letters, and a personal friend of Azuela, Francisco Monterde, has said that the soliloquy of the demented doctor approximates the "interior monologue" of Joyce,[14] and Raymundo Ramos has said that "the interior monologue of the demented doctor constitutes a foreshadowing in the technique of the Mexican novel."[15] The method in this part is not stream of consciousness; the technique is neither soliloquy or interior monologue, even though there may be some resemblance. Contrary to critical opinion, moreover, the madness of the demented doctor seems acceptable, first of all, because he tells the reader twice that he has been in an insane asylum two times, once at the very beginning of this part of the novel (II, 963). Two pages ahead the doctor says that a discussion concerning the difference between killing a man and killing a dog has cost him a second trip to the insane asylum (II, 965). The benevolent doctor's unbalanced mind is not suggested by a chaotic flow of thought or by a confused and disconnected association of ideas. Secondly, the reader is able to grant the doctor's madness because of: his predilection for unusual philosophical and theosophical speculation, concerning himself and Altagracia;

26

his tendency toward strangely poetic disquisition; and his hallucinatory obsession with his dog Lenin, all of which is expressed
by a choppy, fragmentary style. The doctor is, in addition, obsessed with eyes, with his wife's, but especially with Lenin's (as
he remembers them on a medical operating table) and with Altagracia's. In fact, throughout all three of the modern novels, Azuela
exhibits a more than usual fascination with eyes. Eyes are an important leitmotif in all three novels, and this fascination suggests
that Azuela saw eyes as a significant clue to personality.[16]

In this respect the leitmotif of the eyes explains the title of
this second part of the novel and advances a commentary concerning the "dog's life" of Altagracia. For Lenin the dog, in the
mind of the demented doctor, is reincarnated in Altagracia:

> She raised her downy small forehead (a two-weeks
> old donkey) and looked at me. The look of an ani-
> mal, of a domesticated animal, shall we say. It
> turned out that her two firefly eyes in the darkness
> of my room kept me from closing my eyes. I did not
> understand until I got up and opened the balcony for
> her to the splendid night. Lenin's eyes! Yes sir! Why
> not? And theosophy? And Einstein? As far as I'm
> concerned that's enough for me. For me, Universe,
> for me (II, 964).

It is at this point that the doctor begins the account of Lenin, his
dog. This episode, narrated in the first person, is based on the association of Altagracia's eyes with Lenin's in the mind of the doctor. The text of the novel continues:

> By the way, I've not said who Lenin is. A story, the
> day of my triumph or of my downfall, one and the
> same. At ten o'clock the academic welcoming ad-
> dress, at ten forty-five the other. That is to say, when
> under my uniform I could still feel the warmth of
> the embraces and still hear the rounds of applause
> and the intimate fraternal words: "Venerable apos-
> tles of Christian charity . . . noble lives dedicated to

the amelioration of human suffering." And the rest. Why sir, did I have to lay my eyes on Lenin's eyes? Strapped down on the dissecting table, his tense limbs outspread, abdomen facing up, a silvery-grey velvet belly, clammy and perturbed, his breathing heaving in and out with terror. Eyes of glass implacably expressive, overflowing with . . . I don't know. What? Bitter reproaches? Humble and resigned impotence? Plea for the smallest grain of pity? Bewilderment before the omnipotent biped? . . . The heart, consequently, wavered like an untamed bird in a cage. The scalpel would not obey my uncertain hands. But. And the recollection of "sutures for the major vessels of the organism." . . . I turned away abruptly. Lenin's reclining neck, first the incision then the spilling scarlet. And a hoarse bark, suppressed by the mouth muzzle.

* * *

I swear that the rest was not my doing. The surgeon's knife, it cut the straps. Lenin gave a violent leap, broke the window and from the third floor balcony, landed like a sack of bones on the shaded street below (II, 964).

The doctor's obsession is evident in this spoken monologue, quoted extensively because it provides a good illustration of the pathological vision in *La malhora*. But even outside the context of what precedes and follows it, the doctor's monologue, granting that the episode is bizarre, exhibits an orderliness which is also found in the rest of "La reencarnación de Lenin:" a natural forward flow from one detail to the next, causal sequence, rational speculation, the doctor's report of others' views of him. It is a report of a bizarre incident which took place in the past, recreated in the mind, but it leads logically out of what precedes, in this case, the association of Altagracia's and Lenin's eyes. A report of the doctor's institutional commitment, his release, and of a second commitment follows, with an explanation for both commit-

ments. The report borders on soliloquy but the inclusion of dialogue and half-dialogue (as the passages below indicate) in this
part of the novel, with Altagracia and another character Alfonso,
suggest that the doctor is not always alone. It is a first person
monologue with flashbacks. But it is neither direct nor indirect
interior monologue. Moreover, it is, I feel, a less disjointed presentation of an imbalanced mind's inner states than the depiction
of Altagracia's alcoholic mind.

In two other passages Altagracia is associated in the doctor's
mind with Lenin:

> Come closer . . . Don't be afraid . . . Altagracia,
> don't run away . . . Lenin.
> She took a leap and stared at me. A mistake is
> possible. Yet I continue believing in Lenin (II, 965).

And:

> Why do you hide? . . . Look at me! Look me in the
> eyes! . . . And now you're leaving. Wait Altagracia, I
> mean Lenin. Lenin, wait. I must tell it all . . .
> . . . She leaped suddenly and stared at me. Just
> like on the day he leaped over the balcony (II, 966).

Because of Azuela's experimentation with modern techniques already mentioned, the fragmented pathological vision is
convincingly presented. But Azuela makes it difficult to assess
whether one is to understand the whole thing as being all spoken
in *solus,* as a soliloquy must be, or as taking place completely inside the mind of the insane doctor. This part contains ambiguities
which heighten the plausibility of the pathological vision, without ever going so far as to verify it, however. Azuela has said that
he could point to a number of unresolvable puzzles *(rompecabezas)* in all three of his modern novels, but rather than explain
them he preferred to leave them for the entertainment of his ad-
verse critics (III, 1114). That is why the modern novels have also
been called "hermetic."[17] This part also closes with a footnote
supplied by a third person narrator; this adds to the confusion.

Another possible interpretation of this part is that it may be understood as being the doctor's written account (a journal entry, perhaps) of his role in Altagracia's life. But this too remains uncertain.

It seems clear, despite these uncertainties, that with respect to technique Azuela did indeed abandon the clarity and conciseness of his usual manner of composition and narrative methods. Without abandoning certain naturalistic principles or his conventional conception of the novel, Azuela became extremely conscious of craftsmanship, and successful in the use of new techniques to an extent considerably greater than he ever realized. In *La malhora* Azuela's craftsmanship, perhaps influenced by Conrad, led him to alter the conventional focus of narration from the omniscient author to the observer-character[18] (the insane doctor, the shady characters in El Vacilón, and the investigator in the hospital) and to the central character (Altagracia), who is kept by Azuela, like Dionisio in *La luciérnaga,* always in the foreground of the novel's narrative.

The importance of the central character is significant artistically. In fact, the subordinate characters of the three middle parts of the novel are important because of the way they enlarge Altagracia's role as the main character. They help to define the tribulations through which she passes over a period of eleven years on the way to redemption, forgiving, as she does, at the very end of the novel Marcelo, who deflowered her and killed her father, and la Tapatía,[19] who had left her to freeze to death in the park. The third part of the novel, for example, called "Santo . . . Santo . . . Santo," points out the importance of subordinate characters' roles. The title of this part is roughly equivalent to the exclamation "Holy, holy, holy Jesus!" It is an exclamation that comes to the mouths of the two prudish and devout Gutierrez sisters for whom Altagracia works, whenever they are shocked or scandalized by blasphemy or lack of piety. From them Altagracia begins to acquire some religious feelings and compassion. The fourth part of the novel takes place mainly in the home of a retired old Porfirista general and his one hundred and ninety pound sister, Eugenia, a vexatious and intolerably boisterous and demanding person. The old general advances additional information, mainly physical details concerning Altagracia's appearance. All of them supply viewpoints which help develop the main character, Altagracia. In this respect *La malhora* foreshadows the next modern novel, *El desquite,* which uses point of view with even greater consistency.

Azuela's modernism takes still other directions. He employs a combination of stylistic devices which contribute to and compound the complex, fragmented and discontinuous structure of the novel. Also, the narrative of the novel as a whole combines more than one form. It is first of all a chronological or linear narrative. Altagracia is barely fifteen at the beginning of the novel. At the end of *La malhora* eleven years have passed: five at the end of her employment with the Gutierrez sisters (II, 970), one more year before working for the general (II, 971), and five more following that (II, 974). Only in the use of flashbacks or in the character's mental re-creation of a past incident is there a break in the forward flow of the narrative. The best example of the latter is the section of the novel which closes the first part. Altagracia is found naked and nearly frozen in a park, and while efforts are being made to revive her, her consciousness re-creates her confrontation with Marcelo and la Tapatía when Altagracia had attempted to knife him. In this section Azuela has successfully depicted Altagracia's slipping in and out of the state of unconsciousness, her mind alternately dwelling on her aborted act of vengeance (the past) and on the efforts to save her life (the present). In this section Azuela likens her repeated recollection to the repetition of the same film over and over and over (II, 962-63). The same combination of stylistic devices are used here. Azuela's interest in film is noticeable in this and in the other modern novels.

Raymundo Ramos has said of the handling of time in this novel that Azuela contrasts and distributes swift and slow time in the normal flow of this narrative. For Ramos the fragmentation of *linear* time represents for its time an innovative literary contribution.[20] Two other forms of the novel, its quadriform and its cyclical forms, have already been pointed out.

La malhora, then, is important because it clearly brings Azuela from the novel of the Mexican Revolution to the modern novel, to the novel of consciousness. *La malhora,* moreover, points in several ways to Azuela's subsequent development in the next two modern novels. The pathological vision of the benevolent doctor points directly to Jose María in the third modern novel, *La luciérnaga*. Altagracia's alcoholic vision points to both that of Lupita in the second modern novel, *El desquite* (also recapitulatory) and that of Dionisio in *La luciérnaga,* and by contrast to the serene recapitulatory vision of Conchita in the latter novel.

In all three novels Azuela's literary strategy of having central characters recapitulate their lives has the added importance of neatly tying together several narrative strands of the novels. *La malhora,* for all the reasons indicated in this chapter, is therefore of much importance for an understanding of the chronological development of Azuela. It was a stepping stone for Azuela on his way to the peak of his trajectory as a modern novelist. The next stepping stone was *El desquite.*

CHAPTER III

El desquite:
a study of point of view

The happy discovery of *Los de abajo* (*The Underdogs*) in 1925, of which mention has been made, established Azuela as *the* creator of the novel of the Mexican Revolution. In his detailed account of this discovery John Englekirk says:

> So immediate and so widespread was the popular demand for *Los de abajo* that *El Universal Ilustrado* lost no time in availing itself of the golden opportunity for another journalistic coup d'état by publishing the novel in its weekly series. Without previous announcement there suddenly appeared in the January 22 number of the magazine a full-page advertisement proclaiming the publication of *Los de abajo*—"La gran sensación del momento"—in its next issue.[1]

With re-publication, ten years after it was first published in El Paso, Texas, *Los de abajo* hurled Azuela into national and soon thereafter international prominence.

Delighted with this belated critical and public recognition Azuela was encouraged to write his eleventh novel, the second experimental modern work, *El desquite* (*Revenge*). This work began to appear in the 22 July 1925 issue of *El Universal Ilustrado*. In *El novelista y su ambiente* Azuela says:

> And when I most doubted my abilities as a novelist, suddenly and unexpectedly fame came. . . . As could have been foreseen, I lapsed. I wrote *El desquite* using the same technique employed in *La malhora* and more complex procedures (III, 1117).

Of the three modern novels, *El desquite* is the most neglected, and it has never received critical approval. In fact, critical opinion has been unfavorable to this work, and all three modern novels have been severely attacked by Manuel Pedro González who is perhaps Azuela's most impassioned supporter. His critical treatment of Azuela's works is for the most part unreserved eulogy, but González has had the most vituperative words for European avant-garde tendencies. Referring to the period during which Azuela began to experiment with new narrative forms and techniques, he says:

> Towards 1923 mockeries of various European schools or movements began to appear in Mexico . . . particularly of surrealism which had the greatest following. Along with these extravagant, offensive, grotesque and absurd art forms, imagism, metaphorism, and the cult of the word for its own sake were becoming fashionable. The same ships which were bringing us cubist, dadaist, surrealist, imagist, simultaneist, expressionist, ultraist, etc. fashions (novelerías) were also bringing us Sygmund [sic] Freud, already translated, and James Joyce and Proust. For our part we [the Spanish Americans] wished not to be left behind, and Chile contributed "creacionismo," Mexico its "estridentismo," and there were other variants in other countries.[2]

Value judgments notwithstanding, this statement paints a vivid picture of the artistic milieu of the time and underlines European influences on Spanish American letters. González, moreover, shares both Azuela's anguish concerning the imperatives of the times to be modern and the inability of Azuela to appreciate his own experimental works. González says:

> *La malhora* . . . *El desquite* . . . and *La luciérnaga* constitute a trilogy of novels of spurious, borrowed, deliberately imitative and ridiculous technique. . . . In these three novels—so praised by some so-called

critics of snobbish inclinations—everything is fictitious, feigned, and removed from the art of the novel which Doctor Azuela had perfected in previous works. They are based on an artificial and clever formula, imposed by the snobbism of the times, and for this reason, bastardly and without possible legitimacy.[3]

In recent years a reversal of the negative attitude towards Azuela's modern works has gotten underway. But reservations remain, particularly to *El desquite*. Luis Leal, whose fairness to Azuela is beyond question, finds numerous flaws in this work. He says:

> The story is told in a fragmentary, nervous, choppy style. The technique of suggesting instead of telling, of drawing the scenes with blurred strokes, of letting the description stand half-finished, is also that of *La malhora*.
>
> Unfortunately, the technique is wasted on a theme that offers nothing new.[4]

Leal, moreover, feels that the shifts of locale, and the descriptions of the train trips to and from Mexico City are unnecessary and detract from the novel. The ambiguous ending, he feels is weak, and is "perhaps the novel's greatest flaw."[5] His final estimate of the novel is this:

> It cannot be said that *El desquite* is among Azuela's best efforts. He was not able to present a balanced work, as a disharmony is apparent between technique and subject matter, between theme and expression. His style is less spontaneous than in his other novels dealing with the middle class.[6]

And Fernando Alegría in his study of Spanish American literature gives only one passing reference to *El desquite,* and he deals only briefly with the other two experimental novels.[7] Walter M. Lang-

35

ford also dismisses *El desquite* by simply stating that "it is of small consequence."[8]

It is true that *El desquite* contains flaws and that it may not be among Azuela's best efforts. But a close reading of the work, it seems to me, strongly suggests that its greatest flaw is its intolerably overworked and disconcerting style. The style contains excesses which border on offensiveness; it is informed by a trenchant irony and a condescension such as Azuela never exhibited in all of his earlier works. In light of this an immediate dislike for this novel is almost inevitable and understandable. Fortunately these stylistic excesses do not characterize the novel as a whole.

In order to appreciate the worthiness of this novel it is necessary to go beyond these excesses. *El desquite* can no longer be dismissed as negligible. This work builds on the innovations of form and technique of *La malhora* and it adds to the artistic resources which Azuela will bring to bear on his following novel, *La luciérnaga*. *El desquite* works on many levels. In this chapter the aims are to analyze the principle ways in which it reflects Azuela's evolution, and to closely examine its dominant technical and formal elements, but without disregarding its flaws.

In subject matter *El desquite* is not innovative. Leal rightly pointed out that this work, like the earlier novel *Sin amor* (*Without Love*), deals with a marriage based on avarice and contracted without love. Lupita, the main character of the novel, at the instigation of her mother, Mamá Lenita, marries Blas, a wealthy but corrupt businessman who associates with prostitutes and is involved in shady affairs. When Lupita and Blas are unable to have children, they decide to adopt Blas's bastard half-brother, Ricardito, when he is five years old.

Many years later when Ricardito has grown up he schemes against Lupita in order to have Blas get rid of her. Ricardito pumps Blas with alcohol and begins to spread stories, which reach Blas, that Lupita is having love affairs. Ricardito's scheming is aimed at making himself the heir to Blas's wealth when he dies. One day Blas, in his cups, attacks Lupita in a crowded restaurant. In the scuffle he pulls out a revolver which Lupita quickly seizes from him. She cocks the hammer and hands the revolver back to Blas, telling him to go ahead and shoot her if he believes the lies. Blas, overwhelmed by this gesture, gets down on his knees and begs Lupita's forgiveness. On the very next day at his hacienda at San Vicente, Blas either commits suicide or is murdered.

Ricardito publicly charges Lupita with the murder of his half-brother and succeeds in getting a trial set up. The death of Blas and the anticipated trial create a scandal. By this time Martín, who has loved Lupita since she was a child, is a lawyer. At this point he enters the picture as her defense attorney. Inexplicably the trial is called off without Martín's ever having set foot inside the courtroom, and Lupita is acquitted. After this acquittal Lupita and Martín get married.

More than half of El desquite deals with multiple views of the alleged murder, the upcoming trial and its cancellation. At the end of the novel the nameless unemployed psychiatrist who is the narrator of the whole novel, dines with Lupita and Martín. They drink a large amount of wine and the three get very drunk. It becomes obvious to the psychiatrist that Lupita has succumbed to alcoholism and degeneration. Physically and spiritually Lupita has deteriorated; her mind is obsessed with the dead Blas. Azuela never resolves in the novel the mystery of whether Blas committed suicide or was murdered, and if so by whom.

This brief synopsis of the novel sums up the slim story line of El desquite and identifies the main characters. Other characters in the novel are don Crispín, a notary; don Rosario, Lupita's father; don Leodegario, a flour and dry goods proprietor; and don Tiburcio, a merchant. El desquite, in addition, contains short disquisitions on Mexican history and the cult of the Indian, and diatribes on journalism, small village hypocrisy, the medical profession, national customs, miserliness, North American capitalistic intervention in Mexico, and Mexican emulation of French taste.

The revenge of the novel's title, Leal correctly says, is never known.[9] Given Azuela's attitude of having lapsed by writing El desquite, the revenge might very well be aimed at Azuela's reading public and the critics for neglecting his works. Given the irony and black humor with which Azuela has invested these disquisitions, diatribes, and the novel as a whole, this seems an admissible speculation. The title's ambiguity seems to be another of Azuela's rompecabezas intended to entertain and perplex the literati. His sudden emergence into the literary spotlight seems to have propelled him into the writing of *El desquite* with a vengeance.

The commonplace story line, the themes and the characters of *El desquite* obviously do not account for its importance. That they do not, it seems to me, argues strongly for *El desquite*'s strictly formal importance, its modernism. In this novel, Azuela subordinated subject matter to form and technique to a larger extent than in *La malhora.* In some respects *El desquite* resembles *La malhora.* The narrative is fragmentary, episodic and fundamentally chronological. Like *La malhora* this work is also divided into parts, twelve in *El desquite,* and each has a title. They are too short to be considered chapters. They are more like scenes in a play or sequences in a film, and from one to the next they leap ahead in time. With some exceptions they also change in setting. Azuela does, however, supply minimal directives which enable the reader to follow these changes. In some of its parts, also, the novel is more packed with details, sensory and perceptual, then is *La malhora.*

There can be no question but that a deliberate and conscious craftsmanship is at work in *El desquite.* In *El desquite* Azuela carries over from *La malhora* a concern with the depiction of interior states of consciousness. He continues to explore new techniques for rendering them. In *La malhora* the omniscient narrator provided the main focus of narration, but the subordinate characters were allowed to supply points of view of the main character, Altagracia. This method of handling characterization is also used in *El desquite.* But in this novel there is a further development of this method. In *El desquite* the omniscient narrator disappears. Perhaps under the influence of Conrad, Azuela discovered the "dramatized narrator" or "narrator-agent,"[10] the unemployed psychiatrist who narrates the whole story in the first person, with important consequences for this novel.

Azuela's narration of the whole novel in the first person is not innovative; what is innovative is making the narrator-agent's point of view[11] the main focus of narration. Azuela had used first person narration in *Andrés Perez, maderista* and in the first half of *Las tribulaciones de una familia decente* (*The Trials of a Re-*

38

spectable Family). In the latter novel, in *Los caciques* (*The Bosses*), and in *La malhora* first person narration had taken the form of the half-dialogue. In addition, one of the dominant characteristics of the novels of the Mexican Revolution in general was an increased use of dialogue. The innovative use of point of view in *El desquite* means that Azuela was increasingly dramatizing mental awareness. Azuela is following both his own precedent and that of contemporary European writers.

One consequence of the new focus of narration is that character development in *El desquite* is made to hinge upon a single dominant angle of vision, that of the psychiatrist. The choice of a psychiatrist as narrator attests also to the modernism of Azuela. He adds to the clinical method of naturalism, the psychoanalytic method of the modern novel. Multiple points of view of other characters converge upon and are filtered through his consciousness. This use of a single dominant and multiple subordinate angles of vision in *El desquite*, moreover, called for a special handling of time. This is another consequence of Azuela's altering of the novel's focus of narration, with multiple corollary consequences of its own.

In *El desquite* the structural handling of time is twofold. First of all, the story line is developed chronologically, but the consciousness of the psychiatrist is depicted non-chronologically. The story line is episodic and fragmentary, but it begins in the present and ends fifteen or twenty years later (still in the present). Because it is in the mind and seen through the eyes of the psychiatrist that action and plot develop, the story line, like characterization, also hinges upon his consciousness. The consciousness of the narrator, on the other hand, does not follow linear clock-time. Fragmentary, seemingly disjointed and disconnected, it moves freely between the present and the past. Azuela relies on five related techniques to depict the consciousness of the psychiatrist: flashbacks, free association, involuntary memory, the use of leitmotifs and overlapping sensory impressions.

The first part of *El desquite*, for example, illustrates this two-fold handling of time and these techniques. This part begins with a scenic or dramatized description of the psychiatrist's impressions in the mind.

Whistles, wheels, pedestrians, buildings and violent
ringing of bells, the enormous slab of asphalt,
flanked by the woods, dizzily inverted, settled into
place at the Soto Street stop. She then came and took
the seat next to mine (II, 978).

The psychiatrist is travelling aboard a train, and the woman who
gets on and takes a seat next to him is wearing a perfume which is
so offensive that he is forced to stick his head out of the window
until the train begins to move. The perfume, a main leitmotif of
the novel, and the unnamed woman's appearance evoke in the
consciousness of the psychiatrist two contrasting images of Lupita: first, in the vaguest manner, Lupita in the present; and secondly in a more direct way, the child Lupita in the past. The reason
for the present association of Lupita and this woman in his mind
is never developed. Hence it remains ambiguous and unclear. The
memory of the child Lupita, however, is clearly evoked by the offensive perfume, but why it does remains also unclear. The shift
from present to past is illustrated by the end of the first paragraph
and the beginning of the second:

The train resumed its count of rosary beads and I
turned up my eyes contritely. Even though she did
not sense my discourtesy . . . it bothered me. The
child Lupita? Because of the bewildered look of one
on a pilgrimage to the shrine of Guadalupe, because
of the offensive perfume? I doubted. Unsure, I then
unfolded my mute newspaper:
Vacations in the village with my classmate
Martín. Clear morning which opens up doors, win-
dows and hearts alike. Down the solitary street of
ten years ago. . . . And later the satyr-sun swimming
in the little pools of still clear water, in the var-
nished foliage, in the pock-marked houses and in
each string of jewels which the night wept. "Nothing
like the child Lupita's eyes," Martín said. Let's go
then. Mamá Lenita, smiling and pleasant; but I dis-
trust her round eye. A parrot's crossed eyes. Martín,

go easy. . . . There goes Martín with the child Lupita
(Ibid).

At this point the travelling psychiatrist becomes suddenly aware
that the train stops and his thoughts are once again in the present:

> Sudden stop at San Fernando. Once again the noxi-
> ous exhalation of the wretched perfume, harsh
> sounding music at the crossroads. *Imparcial, Mun-
> do, País* and *Nueva Era,* and eyes like lightning on
> the starry blackboard of volts (Ibid).

The consciousness of the psychiatrist which is extremely suscep-
tible to free association and involuntary memory, is directly presented. Sensory awareness in this part is pronounced, particularly
in the continuation of the flashback after the train stop at San
Fernando. In fact, a preponderance of sensory details creates the
effect of overlapping time in the narrative. This is quite obvious, I
think, in the passages just quoted, where they are less preponderant than in the continuation of the flashback.

A related effect which the overlapping sensory details create
is that of simultaneity; present and past impinge simultaneously
on the consciousness of the narrator-agent. For example, the impressions of the psychiatrist at the San Fernando stop, of the perfume, the harsh music, the signs of local newspaper offices and of
electric lights—these lead quite smoothly and naturally into the
continuation of the flashback which is also characterized by ana-
logous, perhaps more intensified impressions:

> . . . below the dome of the lit lanterns winking like
> eyes, stages packed and thundering with opening
> shows . . . Streaming flares against the stars and . . .
> wind music . . . streets ascending, streets descend-
> ing, without rest. "Hot pastri-i-i-e-e-s! Come and get
> your pastries!" Steaming smell of horizontal earthen
> pots lit up like ovens: candlestick sockets of resin-
> ous pine. . . . And Martín slobbering. On the next
> day the grass . . . was damp and the ground smelled

41

fresh. . . . The river bank and the sky in an orgy of colors below the laughter of the sun and the intoxication of the magpies in the ash-trees and the sonatina of the water in the springs. . . . Four ambulatory musicians. . . . The things these huarache-clad ones sing when there's song within. . . . Martín's heart also fluttered isochronized with the panting of the adjacent textile mill, because the child Lupita emerged from the baths with her hair no longer in braids, smelling of Castile soap and fresh water (II, 978-9).

In the remainder of the flashback, Azuela's sarcasm intrudes excessively. This detracts considerably from an otherwise effective cinematic presentation of sensory and perceptual impressions which conjure up a crowded two-day fiesta. He calls it an "annual ambulating pageant of cockroaches and old rats" (II, 979).

The end of the first part brings the flashback to a close and the psychiatrist's awareness back to the present when the train stops once more. The sarcasm is again noticeable:

Stop. Alameda de Santa María de la Ribera. A bull takes her by the arm; a veritable pachyderm who moves his ornate sombrero to the side in order to fit through the narrow door.

And goodbye child Lupita, perfume and all (II, 980).

The same two-fold handling of time and the same techniques are generously in evidence in part ten of the novel, which also takes place aboard a moving train. It is unclear how much time has elapsed up to this point, but the unhappy and childless marriage of Lupita and Blas, the scandal of the latter's death, the passing away of Mamá Lenita, the cancelled trial, and Lupita's marriage to Martín—all these events are behind. At this point Azuela begins to tie together several strands of the novel. The technique is to have the psychiatrist reflect upon the multiple points of view which he has overheard.

Part ten of *El desquite* offers an even better example than part one of Azuela's manner of making the psychiatrist's fluid consciousness respond alternately, first to the passing landscape and the activity and conversation of the passengers aboard the train, and secondly, to events and conversations which took place in the past. On the way to the hacienda of San Vicente where Blas committed suicide or was murdered, the psychiatrist's thoughts turn to Mamá Lenita's sorrow and her passing away:

> The problem of her cruel and obsessed unhappiness focused for me. But I am only going to the hacienda of San Vicente to buy a herd of dumb mules. The hacienda of San Vicente? Yes, it is this matter which reconstructs and sharpens itself for me keeping tune with rotating connecting-rods, with barometric changes, with the single unvaried note of the landscape.
> ... the tragedy no one saw. "Mamá Lenita died of intestinal cancer." Lies, myopic doctors. Her death was a sublimated corrosive which uncorks the retina of the spirit to the black truth. ... Remorse of a mother who, concerned only about her daughter's future, took her fresh and voluptuous flesh to the market. Bless the ... stupidity of mothers who died without ever having opened their eyes (II, 1001).

It is only at this point in the novel that Azuela surrenders the information that Mamá Lenita, who was responsible for pushing Lupita into a marriage without love, has died, apparently of sorrow.

The psychiatrist's thoughts of the past are interrupted several times by conversation and activity aboard the train. After one such interruption he moves from his seat to another and sits directly across from an elderly, motherly woman. As he looks out the window the present and the past fuse in his consciousness:

> Through the little window, irregularly cropped hills.
> ... In the background the mountains with their wigs

43

of . . . cotton. A large field of fragrance passes by . . .
yellow flowers and the heads and flanks of cows . . .

> Madrecita, landscape, murmurs, fragrant
> smells, and Madrecita, landscape, murmurs, and just
> landscape, and . . . the lives of two women, martyr-
> dom of expiation. Lupita, hatching a comedy out of
> two tugging tragedies. "Blas is not a bad man, Moth-
> er. Only a little wild. He flirts like all men his age.
> . . . You exaggerate, Mamá Lenita. . . . If it weren't for
> your habitual sorrow, I would be completely happy"
> (II, 1001).

First the responding of the psychiatrist's mind alternately to the
present and the past, then the simultaneous impingement of
present and past times on his consciousness are illustrated in
these two passages. Involuntary memory is activated and
thoughts of the unhappy marriage, of Ricardo's account of the
scuffle in the restaurant flow into his recollection. The situation
had become so unbearable, reflects the psychiatrist,

> that the pack of wild dogs could not be held back,
> and it led into the intrigues which were to result in
> treacherous homicide. But the savage needed
> crutches of alcohol. That's why he went to demand
> explanations, "stoned." And Lupita? A marvel!
> "Here's the explanation your friends want. Take this
> revolver and kill me. . . ."
> In the blackness of the wind, fine sheet of
> bronze, a musical thunder; with the swiftness of a
> film the sky filled with tempestuous black clouds.
> And the train has halted with the first drops of
> rain (II, 1002).

Passengers are discharged. Farewells are said and presented in dialogue. The psychiatrist's thoughts are once again informed by
Azuela's sarcasm:

44

> Not goodbye, don Manuel, don Ricardo; not good-
> bye, but until we meet again in the hall. Of prehis-
> toric animals (II, 1002).

These passages from parts one and ten illustrate the important role of the narrator-agent's consciousness, which filters the multiple points of view of the other characters and to which he adds his own thoughts.

It seems to me that, far from detracting from the novel or being unnecessary, the descriptions of the train trips in these two parts enhance the plausibility of Azuela's depiction of the psychiatrist's interior states of mind. The effect of overlapping time is made possible by having the psychiatrist's consciousness be attentive to what he sees and experiences while he is aboard the moving train, and to his recollections of the past. Such a depiction of consciousness is faithful to the way the mind really works. More, the movement of the train reinforces the two-fold structural handling of time. Indeed, Azuela has established an effective parallel between the moving train (the present) and the wandering mind (the past). What makes the latter flow sequentially is the use of free association and involuntary memory, which at times create the effect of simultaneity.

Azuela has succeeded in making a single dominant consciousness—the narrator-agent's point of view—serve as the main focus of narration in the novel. The role of the psychiatrist is structurally dominant. By having him dwell on other characters' points of view, Azuela is able to provide an additional, a unifying, perspective on episodes and events already dealt with in the novel.

Equally important as this repetition of the characters' angles of vision is Azuela's method of surrendering information which he had withheld, the death of Mamá Lenita, for example, which is not known until part ten. Azuela uses this method effectively throughout the novel to sustain the reader's interest. By the time the novel reaches part eleven, the characters directly involved in the action of the novel have taken turns in presenting to the psychiatrist their own views and opinions concerning Lupita's unhappy marriage, Blas's death, the scandal to which it gave rise, and other related events and circumstances. It remains for Azuela, at this point in the novel, to give Lupita an opportunity to tell her own story. This she does in part twelve. Part eleven sets the scene and the atmosphere for the last point of view, that of Lupita, who is by then an alcoholic.

Part ten ends with the train's arrival at its destination. The psychiatrist is about to get off. Part eleven starts abruptly with a leap ahead in time and a change of scene, in the manner of a play or a film. This is the only change of setting in *El desquite* for which Azuela has supplied no directives at all for the reader. The beginning of part eleven alerts the reader that the psychiatrist has decided to hear the story—heard from so many sources already—from those directly involved: Martín and Lupita. Parts eleven and twelve are continuous and take place in their home. Part eleven begins with direct dialogue, in this way:

> "Why don't the two of you get away, travel to the United States, South America, Europe?"
> His great surprise and my audacity surprised me (II, 1003).

The three dine and drink to excess. The psychiatrist is very aware of Lupita's deterioration:

> Lethargically, she stretched out one of her thighs, revealing a spongy, ham-like leg at the end of her dress . . . my heart collapsed (Ibid).

He is also aware of Martín who drunkenly smiles and smiles, and of himself:

> And I do not know who I am nor yet what to expect.
> She drank some more. She drank to talk; she was talking to drink (Ibid).

And when she breaks into loud laughter:

> Her loud laughter broke everything up into splinters.
> Then the dim awareness of my surprise and of my

46

failure evoked the memory of a wretched perfume
aboard a train fifteen or twenty years ago. Just like
then I lunged toward the window for air.

There was no perfume. I understood it immediately. But there was the huachichile [Blas] back
from the dead and overwhelming. She was arrogant-
ly fleshy, her chin in rolls, her lips overflowing, bags
under her eyes, boxer's arms, beaver's feet in slip-
pers, gushing her desolation in outcries. *And your
child Lupita, Martín!* Martín, too. His senses
swimming in wine at the edge of his tongue (Ibid).

This passage offers a good illustration of Azuela's technique
of suggesting instead of telling. How the dim awareness of surprise and failure can evoke the memory of the perfume and the
train trip is unclear. Equally unclear and unsatisfactory is Azuela's attempt to objectify Lupita's obsession with her dead husband
by making him return from the dead. But the free association of
the psychiatrist's thought is once again effectively suggested; the
mention of the perfume and the gesture of lunging towards the
window for fresh air make present in the reader's mind, simultaneously, three images of Lupita: Lupita in the present, Lupita associated with the unnamed woman on the train at the beginning
of the novel, and Lupita the child, which the latter association
evoked. All three are meant to be understood as being experienced
simultaneously in the present, in the consciousness of the psychiatrist and of the reader as well.

Azuela, as can be seen, is disturbingly intrusive in the physical description of Lupita. This is also true of the remainder of part
eleven, which deals with the psychiatrist's mental reconstruction
of Martín's life, from indolent student to mediocre attorney, to
ineffectual bureaucrat, and then to defender of the "defenseless
widow" and millionairess, and finally, to husband (II, 1004). Azuela's sarcasm and condescension are frequently disconcerting, particularly in *El desquite*. His characters in this novel are simple-
tons, savages, ploddish, dull-witted, clumsy, stupid, odious, repel-
lent and caricaturesque. Animal imagery is preponderant in his
style. In this novel alone Azuela has likened his characters to par-

47

rot, mule, dog, jackass, pachyderm, bull, chimpanzee, rat, pig, cockroach, beaver, snake and other animals. And Azuela's preoccupation with alcoholism, physical disorders and pathological obsessions, observed in *La malhora* and in earlier novels, reflects his practice of medicine. And yet, says Luis Leal, of Azuela's intrusiveness in characterizations:

> One does not have to think . . . that all characterizations in Azuela ['s works] are negatively presented. Those expressed in positive terms, of normal individuals, are just as common; but it seems that his gift as a creator of characters performs best in characterizations negatively expressed, a gift which one should not deny him as some critics have done.[12]

In the passages from the novel just quoted Azuela seems to be alerting his reader to the final part of the novel. He sets the scene in the home of Martín and Lupita. Then he provides a direct image of Lupita in an advanced stage of physical deterioration—which he juxtaposes to earlier images to heighten the contrast, to underline deterioration and development of characterization—and makes the narrator and Lupita drunk. Part eleven closes with Lupita drunkenly laughing aloud and talking to herself:

> The black-clouded sky began to sob. . . . Martín said to me. . . .
> "Look at her. Her mind." He left us. I never saw him again (II, 1004).

In the twelfth and final part of the novel, Azuela again makes use of a character's summary of events to effectively tie together several strands of the novel; Lupita is allowed to tell her own story. Azuela's consciousness of craft is apparent in the way that he establishes a parallel, as in a film, between a rainstorm building up outdoors and the "storm" gaining momentum in Lupita's mind as she continues to drink. The inescapable flaw in this part is that Azuela makes the beginning of Lupita's sad account coherent and almost serene in order to sustain his parallel. This, of course, is inconsistent with her drunkenness which has already been established.

Modernism in this novel, it would seem, required that technique take precedence over verisimilitude. Part twelve begins coherently:

> The rain drummed lightly on the roofs. The dining room had filled with ash and nauseous shadow. But Lupita, in ecstasy, was looking at the tender gold liquid in her small glass.
>
> "In the beginning I saw nothing but darkness. Who could have been interested in consummating a break which already existed in fact? Only a woman. But Blas had women, and no woman. His life was no secret. And this lasted until the day when I mistakenly opened an anonymously written letter addressed to him. . . . I was accused of a thousand repulsive acts (II, 1005).

She explains calmly that she recognized the handwriting of Ricardito, her adopted son, whom she had loved as her own. Her point of view supplies information by means of which Azuela's characterization of Blas, Ricardito and Lupita is developed. Her account is sad and told slowly. She drinks again and becomes increasingly emotional, but not drunkenly incoherent. She tells the psychiatrist that Ricardito came in through her bedroom window one night and spoke to her of love. When she chased him out the door and down the stairs she discovered that he had brought witnesses:

> "I went for a lamp to show him the way out. Then I saw what had been missing. . . ."
>
> She is interrupted by tumultuous sobbing. The rain fell harder and whipped against the windowpanes. But in the distance the setting sun was still visible in a thread of light.
>
> "The doorman and another man, concealed in the honeysuckle. Witnesses. Do you understand?"

49

The sky opened up and a luminous vermilion sprinkled down like powder upon the trees, houses . . . and even on the bituminous feather-like clouds. Night had been descending. . . .

The murmur of the rain returned, the sky turned even darker. In the distance dogs howled, cows bellowed and the frogs played their immense sonata.

When the lamps came on her anguish immediately lit up.

"Who's there? Who are you? How did you get in? Ah! . . . ah! . . . Now I remember . . . excuse me doctor, but I can't stand so much light. Come, let's go to the study." Her voice was different now, hollow like a broken clay dish (II, 1006).

The parallel is unquestionably melodramatic, the style is overworked. Images and metaphors, particularly in the remainder of this part of the novel, obfuscate meaning, and adjectives are disconcertingly labored. Lupita becomes restless, her mind snaps, but Azuela's depiction of her drunken and hallucinatory obsession with the dead Blas is not successful. *El desquite* ends in this way:

She returned, but her eyes were enslaved. "The other!"

Her tremulous and cerulean finger pointed in that direction. I tried to understand. I dared, "Was it there?"

She was like a hurricane. Her lead limbs wavered like fragile blades of grass. And nevertheless there was nothing. . . .

Her laughter of snow and a sigh bearing the weight of the Universe. She came closer, her hands like iron pincers led my own hand to trace the line which her enormous pupils devoured. And she breathed her hell upon me. "His eyes! Look at them!" (II, 1006-7).

50

The depiction of Lupita's alcoholic obsession with what seems to be the ghost of Blas fails also because it is depicted through the perceptions of the coherent psychiatrist, who is also supposed to be drunk, rather than hers. Her alcoholism is conveyed more by action and dialogue than by a depiction of mental states. What saves the melodramatic ending of *El desquite* is the use of a final recapitulatory angle of vision. Lupita's point of view illuminates information that had been held in suspense from earlier parts of the novel. This device, carried over from *La malhora*, points directly to the next novel, *La luciérnaga*.

Moreover, while it is defective for the reasons indicated, the use of the parallel, between external rainstorm and interior "storms" in this case, is used satisfactorily elsewhere in *El desquite*, notably in parts one and ten, which take place on trains. In these sections the cinematic qualities of the novel are produced by this technique. The parallel technique is also used in parts seven and eight, which take place in a bullfight arena. In these bullfight scenes, parallels are suggested between the activity in the arena and the mental activity of the psychiatrist, and even more subtly between the violence of bullfighting and that of Blas's death. In these arena parts of the novel, a great deal is contributed to the development of the novel by the angle of vision supplied by don Tiburcio. His point of view focuses on the "cold-blooded murder," the trial, and on Martín's role in getting Lupita acquitted, possibly through bribery of the judges (II, 992-6). Throughout the novel, then, on the trains, at the bullfights, in the home of Martín and Lupita, the consciousness of the psychiatrist is highly active, gathering at all times the numerous points of view of the characters. The use of a dominant and multiple subordinate angles of visions account, in part, for the episodic and fragmentary structure of the novel. The importance of the ordering point of view, that of the narrator-agent, is also underlined.

Parts ten, eleven and twelve all refer back to earlier parts of the novel. Through repetition Azuela places episodes and events into a coherent perspective, weaves various strands of the novel together.

Lupita's angle of vision, next to that of the narrator-agent, is perhaps the most important point of view, mainly because of its

51

placement at the end of the novel. All points of view, however, exemplify Azuela's technique of withholding information, of surrendering it in fragments and of episodically building up the narrative. They also show the extent to which Azuela has moved towards showing instead of telling, of allowing much of the novel to speak for itself. Azuela also effectively distributed the partial accounts of the characters; his settings are also partially and ambiguously rendered. Azuela thereby enhanced the complexity and ambiguity of the novel. Where the ambiguity is not the result of stylistic excesses it is a positive trait of the novel.

Of all the artistic consequences in *El desquite*, the use of the narrator-agent marks the most significant advance in Azuela's evolution as a novelist. Azuela found his "focusing center" for this novel in the psychiatrist, in a manner not unlike that of Henry James in *The Ambassadors*. But unlike James, who used the third person, Azuela used the first person narrator. In his use of free association and involuntary memory, Azuela hit upon one aspect of the method of stream of consciousness.

But in the novel as a whole, while Azuela does make the consciousness of the characters his subject, like James, he differs from stream of consciousness writers in that he is concerned with consciousness on a level which corresponds, as Humphrey puts it, to the speech level. *El desquite*, like *The Ambassadors*, lacks the free-flowing quality of true stream of consciousness.[13]

Azuela's discovery of free association is also far from Proustian stream of consciousness. What impresses most about Proust is his method of scrutinizing the object of his memory and the process of memory itself. Proust pursues his memories' movements, their flow and their trails with endless admiration and fascination. Frequently, with considerable effort and patience Proust struggles to bring forth recalcitrant memories, for example those produced by the petite madeleine. Azuela does not make remembering the object of his scrutiny, does not show the trails left by the remembering mind. Azuela, who felt that Proust was inimitable, may have learned to use free association and involuntary memory from him. But Azuela in *El desquite*, was not in command of Proust's method.

Azuela, I feel, succeeded in dramatizing the psychiatrist's

consciousness, in making it the main focus of narration, and in letting the story tell itself. Azuela's artistic achievement in *El desquite* included his two-fold structural handling of time. His use of the narrator-agent also provided him with a means for giving continuity to *El desquite*. It is the consciousness of the psychiatrist which gives unity to the novel's multiple and fragmentary points of view. The use of leitmotifs—the perfume, the eyes, the train, recurrent animal images—this technique also helps to establish narrative continuity in the novel. Each leitmotif serves as a cross-reference in the internal texture of the novel.

Azuela's handling of time, characterization and setting is consistent with his use of leitmotifs. As structural elements of the novel they function as strands that weave in and out through the narrative and also through the consciousness of the narrator-agent. Shifts in time, as pointed out, are sequential in his consciousness. Characters develop according to the way he sees them and from what they tell him. In these many ways, all of which reflect Azuela's discovery of the manner in which experience, settings and action impinge upon human consciousness, there is a commendable craftsmanship at work.

In a final analysis the sizeable flaws of *El desquite* are far overshadowed by its artistic merits. *El desquite* does not surpass *La malhora*, nor is it a lesser novel. In each of them Azuela used similar and different techniques. Together, these two novels enlarged Azuela's artistic resources. The benefit to his craftsmanship is inescapably evident in his third modern novel.

In *El desquite* as in *La malhora* Azuela was interested in depicting mental states and their sensory and perceptual experience as this experience was affected by alcoholic and pathological states of mind. In *La luciérnaga* this interest continues, and the imperative of the times, to be modern, finally propelled Azuela to master several techniques of the modern novel, with which he had experimented in *La malhora* and *El desquite*. This command of modern craftsmanship allows him to turn point of view into visions. *La luciérnaga*, the subject of the next chapter, is a novel of visions.

CHAPTER IV

La luciérnaga:
a novel of visions

La luciérnaga (The Firefly), written in 1926, is the third and
the last of Azuela's modern novels. By 1932, when it was first published in Spain in its entirety, La luciérnaga had been modified by
Azuela to make it less modern, less complex. E. J. Mullen, who
made a brief study of the modifications, says:

> A comparison of the original version of the pivotal
> third chapter . . . which appeared in the controver-
> sial Mexican literary review Contemporáneos with
> its counterpart in the Madrid edition serves well to
> highlight . . . fundamental differences between the
> two. . . . The text of the earlier version contains a
> number of devices of . . . stream of consciousness
> . . . which were deleted or masked in the revision.[1]

Mullen concludes that Azuela "was influenced more strongly
than the Madrid edition hints by avant-garde movements of the
twenties."[2]

Even in its present form La luciérnaga is still innovative in
many respects. In this work, Azuela masters several stream of
consciousness techniques which he had closely approximated in
La malhora and El desquite. La luciérnaga, in technique, foreshadows by many years José Revueltas' El luto humano of 1943,
and Agustín Yañez's, Al filo del agua (At The Edge of the Storm)
of 1947, the latter of which is considered the first truly modern
Mexican novel.

La luciérnaga is a novel of visions. The vision, which goes
beyond point of view, is Azuela's outstanding discovery in La luciérnaga, and his main contribution to the twentieth century
novel of consciousness. In La luciérnaga Azuela develops three

visions with consummate skill: the alcoholic vision of Dionisio, the central character; the pathological vision of José María, his brother; and the serene vision of Conchita, Dionisio's exemplary wife, the "firefly" of the novel's title.

Dionisio, José María and Conchita, the main protagonists of the novel, are among Azuela's favorite character types. Dionisio is the head of a respectable family from the provinces. Out to make his fortune, he moves from Cieneguilla to Mexico City with his wife, Conchita, and their children, María Cristina, Sebastián, and the infant twins Cirilo and Nicolasa. In Mexico City Dionisio is quickly plunged into the squalor, corruption, vices and violence of the modern city. José María, a thief, opportunist and miser, remains in Cieneguilla. And there is a host of shady characters, all of whom descend like vultures upon Dionisio, who brings with him from his native village an inheritance of fifteen thousand pesos: don Benito, self-appointed pharmacist who sets up Dionisio for a narcotics transaction, on pretext of friendship, and ends up swindling him; Chato Padilla, slick automobile salesman who sells Dionisio buses and trucks which too soon end up in the iron and steel graveyards; and shady underworld characters, la Generala, proprietress of La Noche Buena, a bar in El Tepito, and el Chirino, crook and murderer, who recall la Tapatía and Marcelo of *La malhora*. There is don Antonio, a gachupín (a Spaniard), owner of La Carolina Bar, who marries eighteen year old María Cristina only to bring about her degeneration and death in his bar; Father Romero, an opportunistic village priest who goes after José María's hoarded wealth, supposedly for the Church, when José María calls him in for a final confession. There is also Teodomiro, alcoholic ex-municipal judge from Cieneguilla, who appears briefly and inconsistently as a narrator-agent.

As in *El desquite* Azuela is unable to place himself at a distance from his creations. The sarcastic and mocking treatment of his characters, particularly of Dionisio, is perhaps the novel's biggest flaw. Yet Azuela succeeds admirably in depicting his alcoholic vision, and may have surpassed it with the skillful depiction of José María's pathological vision. What makes Dionisio and José María different from any other character in Azuela's work is the striking intensity of their respective visions. To a greater extent than Altagracia and the demented doctor in *La malhora,* and Lupita in *El desquite,* among others, Dionisio and José María are plagued and defeated inwardly. Their painful memories, hallucinations, nightmares, moral conflicts and guilt serve Azuela as vehicles for developing two of the novel's main strands. Most of the action of the novel takes place in the minds of Dionisio and José María. Their two visions and the serene vision of Conchita are instrumental in developing the novel's major themes, plot and characterization.

Azuela's modernism is manifest at the very beginning of *La luciérnaga.* To place the reader inside the consciousness of Dionisio, Azuela uses the indirect interior monologue. When his bus collided with the La Rosa streetcar, Dionisio was hurled to safety. Stunned and under the influence of alcohol and marihuana, he looks upon the carnage for which he is responsible. In a manner reminiscent of Altagracia's drunken recollections, Dionisio recreates the collision in his mind.

> A thunderous noise, clamorous screaming, and stupefying silence. Like a blind bullet the bus had dug itself right into the flank of the red monster, reducing it to slivers. Overturned, the dead beast was smeared with brain pulp and bloody hair. The faint groaning of the dying could be heard within its open belly and among its twisted entrails (I, 567).

Azuela uses the third person but he clearly intends to suggest for the reader what goes on inside Dionisio's mind; it is the "atmosphere of the mind" which Azuela is attempting to convey. *La luciérnaga* is similar to *La malhora* in its use of the omniscient narrator. Consequently, *La luciérnaga* also employs such conventional narrative devices as author commentary and exposition. But Azuela's preoccupation with his characters' consciousness takes him beyond point of view, as in *El desquite,* into vision.

The images of the collision and the carnage become riveted in Dionisio's mind. Throughout the novel, as leitmotifs, they haunt his alcoholic mind. Another Azuela favorite leitmotif, that of the eyes, early makes its appearance. As Dionisio is running away from the carnage, down the Alameda, headed towards the zócalo, he feels panic when a stranger's eyes fix their gaze upon him. There are melodramatic parts also: "stone benches threaten him with wild eyes," the stranger's two eyes multiply into "squadrons marching in time with a hundred explosions a minute," and once he reaches and enters the Cathedral, its interior seems to close in upon him and its statues to mock him (I, 568). Throughout the novel Azuela's use of leitmotifs assist him in depicting mental obsession.

The collision is one of numerous crises in the life of Dionisio and his family since their arrival in Mexico City. Fear of the consequences and drunkenness heighten, distort, and fragment Dionisio's sensory perceptions. Someone leads him out of the Cathedral, and,

> His eyes open and he is alone. In one enormous breath his nostrils flare out, inhale all the air, all the reverberating sun, carriages, tramcars, pedestrians, bell tollings, the Pegasus, the municipal government building, the arcaded porches, the National Palace, all the zócalo and all the sky overhead. "Thank you, Lord! . . . And he stops looking . . . until his bewildered eyes behold the bewildered eyes of Conchita, María Cristina, Sebastián.
>
> "Not a drop, Conchita, I swear, not a drink in a week! But right now I must. Go to the corner, get a bottle of parras. Can't stand it. Can't stand it any more." And Dionisio sinks like an Atlas under the pillow on his cot. Life and time slip back, months, years. Inquisitioner Friar? Keeper of the door to hell? Brother José María (I, 569).

In the above passage there is a completely abrupt leap ahead in time and a change of scene as in a film cut, without any warning or directives whatever. At one moment Dionisio and his family are standing in front of the Cathedral, and at the next they are all at home. In this passage, also, Azuela depicts multiple sensory details impinging simultaneously upon Dionisio's drunken mind.

58

Dionisio remains in his cot, but his mind drifts into the past.

In Dionisio's mind a dialogue takes place between himself and his brother, José María. This dialogue (the past) alternates with repeated references to Dionisio's demands for more to drink (the present). The method here is not unlike that used by Azuela to depict Altagracia's mind coming in and out of consciousness in *La malhora*, and the psychiatrist's consciousness aboard the train in *El desquite*. The use of an omniscient narrator in *La luciérnaga* allowed Azuela to accelerate, retard or develop action through summary and exposition. For example:

> Dionisio kept asking for more drinks. As it got later and later he finally passed out for fourteen hours, from which he was to awaken to the horrible news in the morning paper (I, 572).

Azuela's depiction of Dionisio's alcoholic vision gains in force when the omniscient narrator effaces himself. Also, as in *La malhora*, Azuela described both obsession and action to render states of consciousness. In the remembered dialogue Dionisio's obsession with eyes is stressed again:

> That's it. The same voice as his, José María. I don't know why I never noticed it until now. Not only that. You have the same eyes and that same scowl which used to make us all tremble. Ha! Ha! Ha! Remember José María? How I would run to meet him and kiss his hand, but when he turned his back I would stick out my tongue? Ha! . . .
> You are speaking of our father, Dionisio!
> Yes! That's it. His voice, the same tone (I, 571).

In this passage Azuela conveys obsession with the leitmotif of the eyes and free association. In later parts of *La luciérnaga* Dionisio's alcoholic mind associates the eyes of several characters simultaneously: those of his dead father, of his brother whom he kills, and of his dying son, Sebastián.

Descriptions of actions also enhance depiction of Dionisio's alcoholism. He drinks heavily to bring oblivion, to escape the haunting memory of the collision and the carnage. Here is Azuela's description of the drunken Dionisio, reminiscent of the novelist's description of Altagracia:

> He staggers back from the tavern, announcing his return with crashing doors, chairs, tables and shattered glass. The women huddle defensively in a corner. But there he goes with an open straight razor. The amblyopia of that blood which spills and spurts from an endless stream of corpses being removed from among twisted steel and wooden splinters is a flame which consumes his mind and heart and which will not be extinguished except with many cubes of blood.
>
> The steel flashes in his hand. He is intent not on slashing open the viper's nest in his own brain but the throats of his wife and children who have dashed towards the door yelling for help (I, 572-73).

In this passage Azuela describes both the actions of a drunken man and his mind's vivid obsession. The carnage caused by the collision is brutal and violent in its imagery. Imagery, then, and repetition help to suggest Dionisio's alcoholic vision.

In the first chapter Azuela also uses free association to introduce background information. Dionisio's memories of his brother, of his native Cieneguilla and of bringing his family to Mexico City, contribute to the development of plot and characterization. Following the collision, for example, when Dionisio's family is completely without funds, Conchita goes to Benito, the pharmacist, to ask for a loan of five pesos. The five pesos loan activates Dionisio's memory. He remembers his arrival in Mexico City, that his victimization had begun on the day of their arrival. The hotel where they had stayed, and the restaurant at that hotel, had both charged him exhorbitant prices.

The reference to the five pesos leads the narrative into the past; the reader is installed in Dionisio's memory. After the hotel incident, Benito had offered Dionisio and his familyhis home, but he had ended up "borrowing" one hundred pesos in less than twenty-four hours.

As the narrative continues time is fragmented. It eschews chronological development. The order of events passes chaotically through Dionisio's memory. The reader learns of numerous schemes to separate Dionisio from his rapidly dwindling inheritance. Among the schemes, the narcotics transaction for which Benito had set Dionisio up, had so embarrassed Dionisio that he had never told Conchita. Dionisio's memory, many pages later, brings the narrative back into the present. He reflects on the irony of being lent five pesos, for which Conchita is deeply touched, by a man who had swindled him out of over a thousand pesos (I, 574-582).

In the remainder of the first chapter, it is through Dionisio's dimmed alcoholic perceptions that events and episodes develop in the present. These alternate with numerous flashbacks triggered by associations. As a consequence of the family's financial distress (in the present) Conchita and María Cristina see no alternative but for the latter to marry the lecherous old gachupín, don Antonio, and for the family to move in with him. The wedding preparations are kept from Dionisio who remains continuously drunk.

When Dionisio answers a knock at the door of their house two collectors from the Ford agency come in. They have come to confiscate Dionisio's possessions in lieu of non-payment on two buses which he had purchased. Dionisio remembers, by association, the morning of the collision. Laughing desperately and drunkenly he tells them to take all of his belongings. But his furniture is worthless. They leave and Dionisio breaks down emotionally. He remembers the collision; the recollection of the collision evokes, in turn, still another flashback, hence a flashback within a flashback. The technique, with authorial exposition, is the indirect interior monologue; and this leads into a monologue spoken by a narrator-agent, Teodomiro.

> The collectors from the Ford dealer. The inexorable truth that has suddenly struck his soul. . . . What day? What time? Yes. Only four hours before the col-

lision. Two collectors. With the notice to repossess
the bus if within twenty-four hours four payments
in arrears are not covered. Repossess my bus! My
bus! My bus! All that remains of my fifteen thousand pesos! What will become of my poor family?

Because, to the prank of Benito the pharmacist,
Dionisio had responded, burning with shame, curs-
ing his eternal indecision, on waking up the following day, by running to see Chato Padilla.

Accidently, I was a witness to the transaction (I,
584).

The spoken monologue of the narrator-agent at this point,
even though it adds background information, is completely gratu-
itous. What stands out in the passage quoted, when considered in
its fullest context, is Azuela's unprecedented fragmentation of
narrative structure, his use of several complex narrative techniques in combination, his repeated shifts of the narrative focus,
and the way he eschews the chronological development of the
story line. In these ways Azuela presents vivid and forceful depictions of Dionisio's alcoholic vision.

In the remainder of the first chapter Azuela provides brief
glimpses of María Cristina. Azuela hints at her progressive adap-
tation to metropolitan life, understates the tragic events to follow. Azuela develops parallel strands of the narrative. One strand
which begins with the collision moves ahead, in fragments, frequently in leaps. Another strand of the novel, led by Dionisio's
alcoholic vision, wends in and out of the present. Most of the action takes place in his mind. A third strand, that which is carried
by the pathological vision of José María, also begins to unfold.

The closing parts of the first chapter reveal other misfortunes
which began with their arrival in Mexico City: Dionisio's introduction to marihuana, his increasing reliance on drink, and finally his attempt to kill his family after the collision. Dionisio's attempted killing of his own family produces a violent upheaval in
his mind. This upheaval is presented in the form of a dialogue in
which Dionisio's "other self"—his conscience—argues with him
(I, 591-92). This polarization of Dionisio's mind enables him to ar-

rive at his own rationalized exculpation for the deaths of the collision victims. His upheaval is activated by the morning newspaper's report that his assistant driver, the only one who knew the real story, died without ever regaining consciousness. Dionisio, arguing with himself, finally realizes that he had in fact tried to commit suicide. The collision of his bus with the La Rosa streetcar which killed many people does not make him a murderer; for "obviously a person intent on committing suicide is not a murderer" (I, 592).

The first chapter is important thematically because it presents a great deal of background information concerning the circumstances which bring Dionisio and his family to the precarious situation with which the novel begins. Formally, it is important because it lays the framework for the novel as a whole. Azuela abandons chronological narration.

La luciérnaga has a complex, fragmented, non-chronological narrative structure. Bits and fragments of dialogue, of events, of thoughts, move disconnectedly into each other, guided occasionally by authorial exposition and summary. This new structure exhibits Azuela's handling of time which, as in the two earlier novels, is intended to reflect the way the mind really works. The discontinuous narration of the novel which eschews linear plot development, is thus the technique which Azuela hits upon for handling time structurally. As Raymundo Ramos has said:

> Is it not simply a new way to approach reality, to interpret and render it to take advantage of a double dissection of consciousness and time? Time and consciousness are the materials of the novelist with which to make his analysis. Or, perhaps, it would be best to affirm that the modern novel is constructed on the premises of psychological time, of a subjective flow of time which is, notwithstanding, real.[3]

The second chapter, "La soga al cuello" ("The Noose Around the Neck"), is very short, but it is important. In the first chapter Dionisio's consciousness provides a point of view toward himself and his brother, José María, whom he associates with his dead fa-

63

ther. His own brother had also victimized Dionisio by cheating him of some of his inheritance. In the second chapter Azuela continues to develop the relationship of the two brothers. But Azuela begins to bring the pathological vision of José María into the foreground. In one instance of the second chapter Azuela attempts to convey the simultaneity of Dionisio's thoughts in Mexico City and those of José María in Cieneguilla. In this significant attempt the student of film will recall the cinematic device of cross-cutting perfected by D. W. Griffith and Eisenstein.[4] In Mexico City, Dionisio is thinking of suicide:

> After mailing a letter to his brother, José María, Dionisio returned from the mailbox and threw himself, face down, on his hard cot. He lay there absorbed in the slow passage of time . . . until the answer to his problems came in the form of a clothesline dangling from the ceiling . . . quietly inviting his idleness with dark suggestions. Dionisio's head swinging round, his feet dangling in the air (I, 592).

His wife calls him for breakfast, as he imagines his own suicidal hanging, just as he is about to smoke a marihuana.

> Simultaneously . . . due perhaps simply to a nightmare, José María, in bed, in his own home, in Cieneguilla one hundred and eighty miles away, was visited by a vision of lines, planes and colors, darkened and impoverished by his miser's recollections of a pilgrimage. . . . Meanwhile, in a sombre and nitrous room, Dionisio, his wife, Conchita, María Cristina, Sebastián and the little ones, huddle together in an unsightly precariousness, shivering of cold, with nothing on to conceal their private parts (I, 593).

Immediately following the above passage, Azuela depicts a hallucinatory vision in the pathological mind of José María. He intuits what is actually happening to María Cristina in Mexico City:

64

Suddenly, in an unexpected way, María Cristina, magical, luminous, voluptuous, leaps upon a table amid a storm of laughter, applause, tablecloths, eyes, glasses and silverware. In a fantastic glow of magic paper lanterns, reverberating light, and the play of electrical currents in water, assaulted by a procession of incandescent eyes, she rocks to the rhythm of a voluptuous dance, swimming in a sea of silken waves which exhibit the nakedness they are meant to conceal. Cinematic exaggerations, very likely, in the sleeping celibate mind.

María Cristina will bear the burdens of her family with the strong marble power of her thighs. But like her uncle José María, to date she knows no cabarets aside from those she has seen in movies (I, 593).

The imagery, reminiscent of that used in *La malhora*, points up the afflicted miser's moral conflicts. Again Azuela uses references to film as analogies to the imaginative flow of consciousness. The relationship between Dionisio and his brother, to some extent established in the first chapter, is further developed and brought into the novel's present. The fate of Dionisio and his family now becomes irrevocably linked with the fate of José María through Azuela's technique of simultaneity.

The second chapter, therefore, is structurally significant, for it links the fate of the main characters. It also provides an easy transition from the first to the third chapter, for the second chapter allows Dionisio to recede slightly from the foreground and it brings José María forward.

Azuela's use of Dionisio's letter as a device to develop characterization is extraordinarily successful in the third chapter, "La luciérnaga" ("The Firefly"). The craftsmanship of this whole chapter hinges to a large extent upon Azuela's handling of that device. The letter keeps Dionisio, the central character, always in or near the foreground. And Azuela's use of this device is skillful. His manner of withholding and slowly revealing its contents provokes, as it were, the personality of José María, and brings it into high relief. As a literary device Azuela's use of the letter follows very closely, by almost a hundred years, the model of Balzac in *Eugenie Grandet*, including the use of the miser character-type. Azuela's letter device precedes by two decades an equally masterful handling of the same device by Agustín Yañez in *Al filo del agua* (*At the Edge of the Storm*). In the case of the two Mexican authors the device is used to precipitate intense psychological drama in their respective character's consciousness. Of chapter three in *La luciérnaga* Luis Leal has said:

> The chapter dedicated to the analysis of the miser's moral conflict (he blames himself for the damnation of Dionisio and his family) stands out as Azuela's best novelistic effort. The scene of the miser's agony and death, made tense by the use of a chopped style, is reminiscent of some of the somber scenes of Dostoevsky's novels.[5]

The analysis to which Leal refers depicts José María's agonizing introspection and the distortion of his perceptions and memories due to self-inflicted physical abuses. Azuela endows José María's tormented inner life with power and vividness through the use of multiple levels of consciousness in which time is fragmented. José María, miser, awakens on his thirty-fifth birthday to the tolling of bells for afternoon prayers. Emaciated and sickly because of self-imposed malnutrition, José María is inwardly afflicted. His mind is the battleground for moral conflicts, a screen upon which nightmares and hallucinations flash rapidly.

As in chapter one most of the action of chapter three takes place in the mind. To convey the inwardness of experience, to suggest the mental confusion and unusual anguish of José María's pathological vision, Azuela, without abandoning omniscient narration, skillfully used the stream of consciousness method based on the indirect and direct interior monologue. Here is José María in a state between sleeping and waking:

> An eruption of coughing turned his face red and his prayer turned into a bubbling of blood in his mouth. "This is my birthday present! Blessed be God!"

Then the procession. Procession of mummies, skeletons and phantoms. Dionisio, Conchita, María Cristina, Sebastián, Cirilo and Nicolasa, and even old Watchdog, the deceased dog of the deceased don Bartolo.

José María rubbed his eyes until he was awake. "What? Ah yes, Dionisio! That Dionisio! Where's his letter? What a memory! I think it's in the drawer that's full of junk" (I, 595-96).

José María's states of mind become more delirious and hallucinatory as the chapter progresses. His consciousness is given over to the chaotic play of sensations and associations. Dionisio's letter, the content of which remains undisclosed for several pages, provokes the miser, produces feverishness in him. Dionisio has asked José María in the letter, the reader eventually learns (I, 601-03), for money in order to maintain the decency of his household. José María becomes so emotional that he is unable to respond to his brother.

José María's sophistic speculations, his rationalizations for not sending money to his brother, the thoughts of what he wishes to say in a letter to Dionisio, all point up the miser's pathological obsessions. When his little illegitimate son, a wretchedly dressed and simian looking, beady-eyed boy comes to visit him, José María's self-flagellation and prayers are interrupted. Immediately upon giving the boy a coin, José María is agonized by regrets. By association he remembers that once in the past he had given two pesos in silver to a crying woman with two children, one at the breast. Her husband had just been executed for deserting Villa's forces. The experiences of the past and the present join in his present shame. To him his goodness of heart seems impulsive and unpardonable. In this frame of mind Dionisio's request is all the more repugnant to José María, and he plunges into profound and feverish moral conflicts (I, 596-600).

José María's hallucinations and nightmares are compounded by fever and self-imposed malnutrition. Moral conflicts and bizarre rationalizations assault and torment the miser. José María fails to act, fails to reply to Dionisio. An urgent telegram arrives later from Dionisio; Dionisio tells his brother that he almost committed suicide, and he pleads for immediate help. José María vacillates between sending immediately a hundred or two hundred pesos. Finally—in a direct interior monologue—he rationalizes that to send Dionisio money would be to plunge him deeper into the flames of hell:

> Why does my unfortunate brother suffer? Because of his sins. Well then, where would it be preferable for him to purge himself, in the ridiculous sufferings of this life or in the scorching flames of purgatory? It is barely believable that you, José María, a man of conscience and experience, could aim to deprive your brother of that cross which Our Lord has placed on his back, could dare to deny him the ineffable benefits of the true life. Suicide! A trick to get money out of me! (I, 609).

In this chapter Azuela presents a great deal of background information concerning José María, who had acquired his hoarded wealth through trickery and theft during the Revolution. José María's personality, past and present, is fully developed. At the same time the tragic consequences of the miser's failure to assist Dionisio and his family are glimpsed, Azuela tellingly withholds information about his characters. José María becomes increasingly feverish and pathologically obsessed.

Further along in this chapter numerous people in the village come to the ailing José María with newspapers. Azuela withholds the contents of the newspaper report as he had withheld the contents of Dionisio's letter. Again Azuela suggests rather than tells, by dealing with José María's response to the newspaper report first, and then by revealing the report itself. The newspapers pass from hand to hand, there is whispering and gossip among the villagers. In these pages Azuela presents numerous points of view less directly than in chapter five of El desquite. Here Azuela is concerned with developing the miser's state of mind rather than the points of view of the villagers. Azuela directly presents these thoughts of José Mariá:

They have been like murderers who came with a
crucifix in one hand and a dagger in the other. First
they show me the headlines, which is like grabbing
me by the neck and burying me in the sewers. When
I am being asphyxiated and beg for air and light,
they, with their pious voices, plunge the knives of
each paragraph deeper emphasizing the most painful
sentences (I, 611).

José María is made painfully aware by the newspapers and by his
neighbors in Cieneguilla that María Cristina, Dionisio's daughter,
has been murdered in a brothel during an orgy attended by several
high government officials.

In his mind José María develops a letter which he writes but
never mails to Dionisio. Here is part of that letter:

I trust that in these words, brother of my soul, God
will not permit you to see bad intentions or worse.
But it is to your advantage to know that the punish-
ment of the Lord for all those who fix their eyes only
on earthly goods is to leave them blind to everything
which is not miserable money. Beware Dionisio! In
the clock of time our hour has tolled. . . . In any case,
come, to satiate your thirst for gold and wealth;
come for the two thousand five hundred and seventy
eight pesos and thirteen centavos which rightly be-
long to you (I, 613).

But José María's thoughts are impulsive, like his generosity had
been. He believes his letter to represent one of the greatest and
most heroic acts in his life:

But as he passes his wet tongue along the glue of the
envelope something like a scruple rises from deep in
the pit of his stomach. What if, in the heat of im-
provisation, some tell-tale word or sentence has
slipped past.

He re-reads the letter . . . his face contracts violently . . . he crosses himself (Ibid).

69

José María feels that his hand has been guided by the devil himself. The letter is too revealing of his arrogance and hypocrisy.

The days, for the miser, become more and more intolerable, and the nights drag on interminably. María Cristina visits him in a nightmare to torment him. His death becomes more and more imminent. He calls a priest to make his last confession, and the priest urges him to consider that both his brother, Dionisio, and the government are ready to leap at the miser's unfinished business. The priest suggests making a will leaving José María's wealth to the Church. The miser, in the throes of death, asks him to leave. When his illegitimate son returns, José María tells him to bring a notary. José María knows that he is dying. His mind is torn between restoring to Dionisio the money of which he has cheated him and wanting to leave it all to his illegitimate son in one final desperate act.

Azuela leaves the final pages of chapter three sketchy and ambiguous. The child arrives with the notary, don Federico, to whom José María dictates a last will and testament. He admits that the boy is his child and tells don Federico that all should go to him. But the notary is uncertain of whether José María is of sound mind. Azuela does not indicate whether the notary accepts José María's last wishes as legal.

The narrative moves ahead. José María, whose mind is dreamlike and chaotic by turns, becomes fully aware that he is dying. Dimly he senses the presence of someone familiar; the departure of the notary is not indicated:

> "To him. Everything. He is my son." He loses the sense of time. Remembering his repeated offenses, he still has tears to shed. The idea that suffering and only suffering, which burns the soul, can cleanse it, took root. He abandoned himself to suffering . . . and in one supreme act of grace, he pleads for more suffering from God. And God hears him. "I must go now, and there is no one to hand me my clothes."
> Even though his cardboard larynx is obstinate in denying the passage of air . . . his ears acquire an extraordinary acuteness. That's why in the voice of the

one who stands in the doorway he recognizes immediately something which belongs to him. . . . What
can I do for you? "Oh! it's you. I'm sorry. You're late.
Well, please hand me my clothes. Do you know that
today I set out on a journey?" (I, 621).

Azuela withholds for a while the identity of the visitor. José
María recognizes his brother Dionisio. Azuela vaguely suggests a
struggle; he depicts José María's mind dimming. José María expresses gratefulness for additional final suffering. But there is no
clear description of the miser's death; in fact:

José María is not able to distinguish whether the
babbled curses come from the mouth of his brother
or issue from the dam of his own conscience (I, 621).

José María's states of mind are obsessed and delirious. His
consciousness pursues chaotic sensations and associations.
Above all the chapters in *La luciérnaga,* chapter three best exem-
plifies the way in which Azuela, in this most modern of his three
experimental works, developed characterization through depiction of mental states, and from the character's thoughts, speech,
impressions, memories and other sensations.

In the fourth chapter of *La luciérnaga* Azuela uses the same
techniques to deal with the consequences of Dionisio's murder of
his brother on both himself and his family. The fourth chapter,
"Los ofidios" ("The Vipers"), once again takes up the alcoholic vision of Dionisio. Whereas the earlier chapters establish a number
of relationships among the characters and supply background information, chapter four begins to deal more emphatically with
the progressive physical and spiritual degeneration of Dionisio in
the present. But the past continues to assault and to haunt him.

The murder of his own brother produces in Dionisio a violent
self-confrontation. Guilt feelings from his obsessed recollection
of the collision which killed many people, his fear of being discovered, his dimly perceived awareness of María Cristina's death,
his drinking, all push Dionisio into an alliance which is to end
disastrously. Dionisio's agitated state of mind is depicted by
Azuela in this manner:

If during the day Dionisio drowns himself in the din
and clamor of La Noche Buena, no sooner does his
head hit the pillow than a wretched dance begins.
Night without drink, night of torments. Procession
of accusing eyes, those of the mysterious man on the
bus . . . the two inextinguishable little flames in the
eye-sockets of a skeleton, "my brother, José María";
the eyes of la Generala, perforating like a hole-
puncher; those sweetly closed of María Cristina (I,
633).

Dionisio's memory of killing his brother becomes an obsession.
Only a confession can unburden Dionisio of the anguish and
guilt. One night, when he is very drunk, he confesses to la Generala, the woman with whom he is to become partners in the pulquería, La Noche Buena. It is several pages into chapter four before it becomes clear that Dionisio has killed his brother (in chapter three):

> I swear before God . . . that I am innocent. I don't
> know what I did, nor how I did it. My own brother!
> He looked at me with those eyes! Can you imagine,
> señora, the living eyes of a dead man? I hate eyes,
> his, those of the other, yours . . . yes, I said yours.
> Stop looking at me that way . . . I forbid you and the
> world to judge me! . . . is it not true that . . . God will
> forgive me because . . . I was out of my senses? I
> think I threw myself on him . . . I think he tried to
> defend himself. A terribly ridiculous struggle, un-
> derstand? Ha! ha! ha! I'm sure that I knocked him
> from the bed to the floor, and that is precisely where
> he croaked. Ha! ha! ha! (I, 634-35).

Dionisio seeks oblivion through heavier drinking and marihuana. With the money which he took from his brother after killing him, Dionisio becomes part owner of La Noche Buena. His
son Sebastián becomes very ill, but all José María's wealth, now in
Dionisio's possession, cannot restore Sebastián's health. Conchita

72

takes Sebastián to several doctors but not one is able to cure him. Having gone to so many doctors, Sebastián, dying of tuberculosis, one day simply refuses to see another doctor:

> Unexpected disobedience. Dionisio takes a step back, raises his voice and even a hand. But his eyes light upon the living eyes of a dead man. The same! The same eyes! The horrible image shakes him momentarily. José María, his dry skin clinging to the bones, his hollow cheek bones, the dark eyesockets and the bright flickering of two little flames (I, 642).

In the remainder of chapter four Dionisio's alcoholic vision becomes increasingly obsessed. Azuela exhibits an artistic control in the depiction of Dionisio's consciousness equal to that which characterizes José María's pathological vision. As in the case of José María in chapter three Azuela effectively underlined the chaotic workings of Dionisio's mind through his non-chronological handling of time. The techniques in the remainder of the chapter are also the direct and the indirect interior monologues.

There is, moreover, one extremely important method which Azuela used throughout *La luciérnaga* to add plausibility to his depictions of states of mind and to increase the effectiveness of his modern techniques. Throughout the novel, Azuela's method was first to suggest vaguely some significant or powerful event in the lives of his characters and then to examine its psychological consequences in their emotional lives and their retrospective understanding of such an event. For example, Azuela suddenly springs upon the reader the following statement:

> The funeral was attended by el Chirino, don Chole and the pharmacist, Benito (I, 644).

This statement comes after an episode which Azuela simply leaves incomplete. It is followed by conversation between the men and Dionisio at the cemetery, and by a lengthy interior monologue in Dionisio's mind.

The death of Sebastián, and that of María Cristina which it brings to Dionisio's mind, produces in Dionisio a redemptively oriented introspection. His introspection provides one of the first extensive points of view on Conchita; Azuela again brings one of his characters into the foreground before he begins his more extensive analysis of personality. So strong is Dionisio's determination to make amends with his wife, and so deeply introspective are his thoughts, that he does not realize that for at least fifteen minutes he has been standing in front of his house, and that Conchita does not answer. A neighbor finally tells him that Conchita has left with the twins, Cirilo and Nicolasa.

At this point Azuela deals with the unreliable memory of the alcoholic Dionisio. For Dionisio cannot understand until a second drink how Conchita's leaving came about:

> A second cognac breaks through the tenuous curtain and from afar the memory begins to take shape. Faded, blurred. It seems to have happened this way. When Sebastián was gravely ill. He arrived as he did every night, half-drunk, half-conscious. "Dionisio, our son is dying!" Hum! A daily nip. Tell me how much money you want and let me sleep in peace. Then she moved back, humble, mute, submissive. . . . But . . . she halted . . . there was strength in her voice. "Dionisio, if Sebastián dies, you will never see me again in your life." They have abandoned me! (I, 646-47).

Chapter four ends with another traumatic and shattering experience for Dionisio; after realizing that Conchita has abandoned him, he returns to La Noche Buena. He discovers that la Generala has robbed him, leaving a worthless check for him. By this time Dionisio's spiritual and physical deterioration is almost complete.

Azuela's method of tracing psychological repercussions in his character's emotional lives, experienced retrospectively, as in this example, is extremely significant in *La luciérnaga*. Conchita's serene vision—the third central vision of this work—offers another excellent example of this method, perhaps the best. Because in the fifth and final chapter, Azuela, with consummate skill, brings several strands of the novel together by making them converge on Conchita's serene vision. In this manner he gives *La luciérnaga* a unified total configuration.

This last chapter, "Naúfragos" ("Shipwrecked Victims"), is itself divided into four parts which reflect many of the novel's outstanding methods and techniques. Part I allows Azuela to lyrically conjure up provincial life in Dionisio's native village, Cieneguilla, to which Conchita has returned with her two children. The theme of this part is time and memory, and it is Proustian in treatment. The effects of time's passage are described lyrically; time becomes arrested and fixed in objects, in memories and in sensory impressions:

> "My native village! Home!" A pure, diaphanous, deep blue. Evocative, too, the river of the village, mirror of its motionless adolescent hours, framed by trees and clouds. . . . Ineffable ecstasy in the caress of wind made fragrant by pollens and resin which dilate the lungs (I, 648).

And:

> She struggles, from the very day she awakens in the village. She awakens in the silence of other roosters' crows, other dogs' barkings, without the incessant droning of the trains at San Lázaro, nor the burdensome whistle sounds of the factories and shops; unfamiliar or forgotten silence (I, 649).

In the serenity of the village Conchita experiences a strange and sweet feeling of consolation:

> Until some unexpected incident, a memory is evoked by a gesture, until a sound or a smell bring back what she believed to have been buried forever. Then she would understand the why of those inexplicable longings to weep which come upon her suddenly . . .

75

Dionisio? A word, a symbol. The father of my
children. Nothing more. . . . Dionisio has been ex-
pelled from her mcmory; a defensive mechanism . . .
just as one expels the memory of a moment, of an
hour, and even of a whole period in one's life when it
afflicts the spirit (I, 651).

In part II of chapter five Azuela develops Conchita's recapitulatory point of view. Her serene vision is activated by a newspaper
report of an assault on Dionisio's life in Mexico City and of his
hospitalization. Villagers like those who brought to José María
the newspapers with the report of María Cristina's death, bring to
Conchita the newspaper with news of Dionisio's hospitalization.
Her memory conjures up her family's trials and heartaches in
Mexico City.

Conchita's sweeping point of view (I, 654-660) is panoramic
in dimension. Consequently it gathers several strands of the
novel and neatly weaves them together. Conchita's vision, for example, rounds out in an admirable way the sketchy personalities
of Sebastián and María Cristina. Her serene vision, moreover, enlarges the character of Dionisio, and absolves him, in her view, of
the responsibility for his deterioration. Conchita assigns the
blame on vice and corruption in the modern city. With compassion and sadness Conchita reviews in her consciousness and in
her conscience the details of hardship years in Mexico City. She
looks back over the circumstances which brought Dionisio to alcoholism and to drugs, to the fatal collision, and then to his
downfall:

Who gave Dionisio the first glass of liquor? Chato
Padilla with his first deceit; then each one of the de-
cent citizens from our village, in uninterrupted sequence. On top of that, the bureaucrats who left him
almost with only the shirt on his back . . . taxes,
fines, and bribes. Drinking heavily, yes, but not yet
an addiction. When he owned the bus which he
drove himself for six months he knew nothing of
pulque or aguardiente. But then came the debts, en-

tanglements, calamities and shame, and then it is hard to know if one drinks because of the evil which others do to one or because one does evil. The collision of the bus where Puente de Alvarado turns was simply the crown on a work of infamy: the defeat of a man not up to being one (I, 655-56).

Conchita is compassionate towards her husband, and understanding about his misfortunes and their consequences for the whole family. Her vision—in which Azuela's presence is strongly felt—places in a calm perspective most of the significant events with which the novel deals. Implicit in Conchita's point of view, moreover, is her own point of view of herself. She recognizes that as an exemplary wife she had always made herself subservient to her husband. She would not complain or judge, she would remain silent and weep privately over their misfortunes. Looking back on her passivity as a mother, and reconsidering its consequences for her dead children,

> remorse of which she always felt herself immune suddenly surges in tumultuous assault. . . . What she had considered virtue in herself, therefore, begins to seem her gravest shortcoming, her greatest sin (I, 657-58).

After a thorough self-examination, Conchita resolves to be strong, and she decides to return to Mexico City, to Dionisio's side.

At this point part III of chapter five picks up the narrative where it had left Dionisio, shattered by la Generala who had run off with his money. The strand of the novel which Azuela now picks up deals with Dionisio's final descent, literally down into the garbage cans and the gutter, and close to his death at the hands of el Chirino. Bringing Dionisio up to his hospitalization this strand of the novel leads into part IV and converges with the strand of the novel carried by Conchita. At the end of the novel Conchita and the two children meet Dionisio at the hospital where he has just been discharged. The novel does not have a happy ending, but it ends on a note of optimism and hope.

In the final chapter then, through the use of Conchita's serene vision, Azuela successfully pulls in several strands of the novel and neatly weaves them together. The effectiveness of Azuela's method of having his characters glance back over a life of misfortunes, remorse and bitterness, to place numerous tragedies into a calm perspective endows *La luciérnaga* with artistic unity.

La luciérnaga, a modern novel, does indeed present points of view which deviate from the ordinary perception of things; they are visions. To depict states of consciousness other than ordinary, characterized by obsession, hallucination, fantasy; to render perceptions, thoughts and impressions tainted or colored by alcoholic or pathological states of mind; to dislocate time, and to dramatize his narrative, Azuela was compelled to experiment with and to use narrative forms and techniques of the modern novel as it was evolving internationally.

Azuela's characters may still fall into the category of types, but, in addition *La luciérnaga's* inwardly defeated protagonists reflect Azuela's concern with the afflicted vision of modern man in a modern world. The pathological vision of José María has been compared in its sombreness to like depictions by Dostoevsky. It is, moreover, not any less effective than other comparable depictions by such writers as Huysman, Hesse, or Mann, among others. With respect to the alcoholic vision, there is a study yet to be written. Zola, Hemingway, Fitzgerald, and Donleavy, among others, have dealt with alcoholism. But it is Malcolm Lowry who has given the alcoholic vision its superlative expression, in his novel *Under the Volcano*, and also in *Dark as the Grave Wherein My Friend Is Laid*. Azuela's psychological analysis of his characters allows them to develop from significant crises or events in their lives, from the impact of these crises, and from the reactions they produce and provoke.

The structure of *La luciérnaga* is fragmented, nonchronological, and seemingly chaotic. In this, the novel's structure conforms to the complexity of mental thought, of memory, and of the actual flow of time in consciousness. Concerning the technique of *La luciérnaga*, Azuela was compelled, if he was to depict the consciousness of his characters—if he was to evolve as a novelist—to explore and master stream of consciousness, interior monologue, free association, involuntary memory, leitmotifs, as well as point of view. The structural handling of time with which Azuela was forced to grapple by using these techniques posed for him the problem of narrative continuity.

Azuela resolved the problem of narrative continuity, first of all, with the method mentioned above, which consists in suggesting some significant event or crisis and then allowing it to develop in all its amplitude in the character's mind, or to be reflected in its consequences or in the character's actions. The collision with which the novel begins is a good example of this method. Azuela leaves strands of his novel dangling (in a positive sense) and picks them up later. Another outstanding use of this method is made at the end of the third chapter. Dionisio arrives just as José María is dying and kills him. Azuela leaves Dionisio's act ambiguous and unclear to the reader. It is only pages later, well into the next chapter as was pointed out, when it becomes clear that Dionisio has killed his brother. Another example is provided by the scene of his son's death, also pointed out already. When Sebastián dies, Dionisio is drunk, and it does not dawn on him until another day when he returns from the funeral, and learns that Conchita has left him. Other examples could be cited, among them, the death of his daughter, María Cristina, in a brothel (I, 611); and the awareness of his own suicide attempt long after it took place (I, 592).

The second method for establishing continuity in *La luciérnaga* is the use of the leitmotif, closely connected with the preceding method. This method and the use of the vision are among Azuela's most skillfully used discoveries in *La luciérnaga*. The leitmotifs weave in and out of the narrative, giving it continuity. One of the main leitmotifs pointed out in this study is the eyes with which Dionisio is obsessed throughout the novel. Another leitmotif is the newspaper which links throughout the narrative the recurrent references to the fatal collision and carnage. At the very end of the novel it is a newspaper that brings the news of an attempt on Dionisio's life to Conchita in Cieneguilla. It serves to trigger in her mind, as pointed out, a recapitulation of the events that crushed Dionisio and led to his spiritual and physical degeneration. In this manner several strands of the novel are neatly tied together.

An equally important leitmotif is Dionisio's letter urgently requesting help from José María. As a structural device, this letter, the content of which Azuela allows gradually to unfold in José María's mind, and to which he reacts emotionally and even violently, is extremely important in the third chapter, for the numerous reasons already indicated. The letter, in addition, and the newspaper which brings to Conchita the news of Dionisio, maintain Dionisio always in the foreground, as the novel develops. Conchita's serene and compassionate recapitulation of events, and both Dionisio's letter and José María's hasty response (never mailed)—which he mulls over and modifies in his mind—install the reader in the consciousness of these characters. Each consciousness interprets the events and the episodes of the novel's story and focuses the characters' points of view on each other and on the various situations. Notwithstanding the novel's discontinuous narration, its fragmentation of and shifts in time, its use of stream of consciousness and other complex techniques, Azuela skillfully resolved with these two methods the problem of narrative continuity.

All of the elements of the novel in the end are harmoniously tied together. Working in harmony they give to the novel its structure and a rhythm in keeping, as Ramos says of *La malhora*, with the contrast of swift and slow time, which itself is consistent with the actual experience of time.

Ambiguity and complexity in *La luciérnaga* enhance its modernism. Some of its "hermetism" is due to Azuela's suppression of syntactical connectives and withholding of information, to his dislocation of time and to his use of several techniques in combination. The frequent effacement of the narrator and the withholding of information account for the incompleteness of certain descriptions, Dionisio's murder of his brother, for example.

In many ways the reader's role is considerably enlarged. Likewise, in *La luciérnaga* the reader enjoys a more participatory role because Azuela based characterization on point of view. In the traditional novel the omniscient narrator supplied all the information about his characters in blocks and arranged his narrative chronologically. In *La luciérnaga* the reader is installed in the consciousness of Dionisio, José María, and Conchita. He shares their perceptions. *La luciérnaga*, therefore, is a modern novel of consciousness; a novel of afflicted visions.

La luciérnaga is also a novel of the modern city. Its setting, in addition to Cieneguilla, is once again El Tepito, the slums of Mexico City. But while its setting is Mexico City, the capital of Mexico, *La luciérnaga* shares its bleak vision of the modern metropolis with works by such writers as Balzac, Dickens, and Zola. Azuela's harsh and sordid images of Mexico City are comparable in force and expressiveness not only to European city images, but they foreshadow, and according to some critics surpass even those of the Mexican novelist, Carlos Fuentes.

In many ways, then, *La luciérnaga* is a modern novel. It is a modern novel of consciousness, a novel of afflicted visions; it is a novel of the city; and it is a novel of time and memory. "In this novel," says Ramos, "one can observe . . . the novelist's desire to evolve in accordance with the taste and sensibility of his time, without blameable concessions that betray his conception of the novel."[6]

"Without blameable concessions;" the truth of this statement is both remarkable and strange, for Azuela, as the conclusion of this study will point out, never permanently modified his theoretical conception of the novel. Following his experiment in technique Azuela unfortunately returned to the novelistic methods and techniques of his earlier novels; he says in *El novelista y su ambiente:*

> After . . . *La luciérnaga* . . . I made a serious and careful examination of my conscience. . . . I was ashamed of having used the well-known trick of overworking words to make them seem intelligent, artistic, and ambiguous (III, 1118).

Azuela, then, abandoned the modern novel. His *craftsmanship*, as evident in *La luciérnaga* in particular, in all three modern novels as a group, was never surpassed in novels which precede or follow the modern works. These three modern novels—*La mal-hora, El desquite* and *La luciérnaga*—attest to Azuela's awareness of the imperatives of the height of the times: to deal with the atmosphere of the mind, and to evolve as a novelist through the exploration and use of avant-garde artistic forms and techniques.

Almost at the end of his life Azuela admitted that he did not regret his incursions into the modern novel (III, 1121). Indeed, the deliberate and skillful craftsmanship at work in *La luciérnaga* has earned it a place among Azuela's two or three best novels, along with *The Underdogs* and *The Trials of a Respectable Family*.[7]

So, notwithstanding Azuela's almost desperately frivolous attitude of having tried to pull the wool over the critics' eyes, which attitude finally led him to abandon the modern novels, Azuela achieved considerably more than he ever realized. To fully appreciate the significance of the modern novels it is now necessary to examine their collective importance. To make this examination, placing them in a larger context, and to make a fair re-appraisal of Azuela's art—these, then, are the aims of the last chapter of this investigation.

CHAPTER V

The art of Mariano Azuela: a re-appraisal

The many modern artistic merits of *La malhora, El desquite,* and *La luciérnaga* discussed in the preceding chapters attest to Azuela's novelistic evolution beyond his novels of the Mexican Revolution. The evidence of deliberate and careful craftsmanship, and of a compelling preoccupation with experimentation and innovation of techniques in these works is considerable. In light of this evidence, one cannot but declare that with *La luciérnaga* Azuela reached the peak of his trajectory as a novelist. Azuela, then, is distinguished from his predecessors in the development of the Mexican novel of the twentieth century by a much greater preoccupation with matters of craft. Contrary to established critical opinion this makes Mariano Azuela, and not José Revueltas or Agustín Yañez, the first Mexican novelist of the twentieth century to employ narrative forms and techniques of the modern European novel.

Mariano Azuela is the first modern novelist of Mexico in the twentieth century. *La malhora, El desquite* and *La luciérnaga,* like his novels of the Mexican Revolution, "bear the unmistakable stamp of their time," as Azuela said of two novels of Rafael Delgado (III, 628). To say, then, that Azuela felt the compelling force of the height of the times, that he was touched by the modern spirit, and that he was influenced by attitudes and principles of avant-garde artistic tendencies arriving from Europe and North America is only to say that he belonged to a definite place in time.

In the preceding chapters this investigation has pointed out that the modern novels obey several principles of modernism. These works, for example, exhibit a decided preference for interior reality, which requires in the novel depictions that more accurately reflect the way that the mind really works. *La malhora, El desquite* and *La luciérnaga* also reflect Azuela's experimentation

83

with new narrative forms and structural techniques. The novels then, give generous evidence of Azuela's having faced the urgent problem of handling time structurally and of having successfully depicted consciousness and the flow of thought. This led him to master the narrative methods of point of view and stream of consciousness, and the technique of the interior monologue.

Like many of his European and North American contemporaries Azuela was abreast of developments in other arts and in artistic and critical theory. Such European tendencies as cubism, futurism, imagism, dada, surrealism, and Mexican *estridentismo* left their mark on the three modern works: in their fragmented and discontinuous narrative structure, the suppression of syntactical connectives, the emphasis on the image, the shattering and re-assembling of forms to create new structures, the dislocation and overlapping of time, simultaneity, and the attention given to the dynamism of technology and modern life, among other things.

Exploring ways to alter the focus of narration in his three modern novels, Azuela also evolved towards the dramatized novel. As Azuela moved forward toward *La luciérnaga*, he went from telling to showing, from statement to inference, from exposition to presentation, from narrative to drama, from explicit to implicit, from idea to image.[1] Azuela's dramatization of the modern novels suggests, in addition, the unmistakable influence of the theatre and the film.[2] Particularly in Azuela's handling of characterization through increased use of dialogue and the half-dialogue rather than block characterization, beginning with the novels of the Mexican Revolution, and subsequently through the use of extensive recapitulatory monologues and point of view in the modern novels, the indebtedness to the theatre in which Azuela had a life-long interest and into which he made some excursions seems patent. His characterization in the three modern works, consequently, is more dynamic.

In this dynamic handling of characterization there is also evolution in method and in the structure of the novel. Azuela had learned his method of characterization from Balzac and Zola, and in the novels of the Mexican Revolution the nature of the circumstances dictated it. The method consisted of quickly jotting down bits and fragments of information and conversation which he saw and overheard, of rapidly sketching into notebooks the more noticeable characteristics, physical details and mannerisms of interesting persons. This method usually began with his following some interesting person whom he saw and sketching him directly from life. He frequently combined details of more than one person. This method carried over into his descriptions of directly observed scenes, pictures, situations and events. This method and the influence of theatre, I feel, account for Azuela's eventually giving his novels of the Mexican Revolution an increasingly episodic and fragmentary structure, from which he evolves ultimately towards the non-chronological, discontinuous narrative structure of *La luciérnaga*. In this manner Azuela was able to retain in his novels the immediacy, directness and spontaneity of directly observed reality, the dramatization of which reaches its maximum expressiveness in his novels of consciousness. His characters, however, remained always types for which Azuela had an unwavering and unshakable predilection.

Other narrative devices which affect the structure of the modern novels, also foreshadowed in the novels of the Mexican Revolution, suggest the combined influence of the theatre and film. This influence is reflected not only in references to these arts contained in the novels but also in the way that Azuela leaps ahead in time or abruptly changes the setting without alerting the reader, and in the modern novels, in the way that he rapidly "cuts" from scene to scene or episode to episode. The influence of film is strongly suggested by the kind of continuity which Azuela gives to the modern works through the use of free association, parallel development and flashback. He came very close at times to the film techniques of cross-cutting and montage.[3] Some examples in which Azuela approximates cinematic continuity are the scenic presentations of the train trips in *El desquite* and the leap which Azuela makes in the second chapter of *La luciérnaga* from the consciousness of Dionisio to that of his brother José María. The cinematic qualities in *La malhora* of Altagracia's drunken vision, as pointed out, are very forceful.

A more conventional device which suggests the influence of the film is the way that Azuela sets the scene at the beginning of all three of the modern novels. There Azuela puts the reader at the scene as in a film long shot, after which he introduces his characters as in a close-up. He did this with great skill at the very beginning of *Las moscas* (*The Flies*). Sometimes he provides the reader with a "sound-track," as he does at the beginning of the tenth part of *El desquite* and in parts of *Las tribulaciones de una familia decente* (*The Trials of a Respectable Family*); Azuela does this by eliminating such directives as "he said."

For all these reasons the modernism of Azuela cannot be questioned, nor the considerable extent to which he evolved in accordance with the dictates of the modern sensibility. Along with these many changes in the practice of his art, moreover, by dramatizing his modern novels, Azuela ultimately modified the roles of the narrator and of the reader. By de-emphasizing the former Azuela invited the reader to vitalize his imagination and to become a more active participant—a co-creator, so to speak—in the re-creation of the novels.

It cannot be stressed enough, however, that Azuela never permanently modified his theoretical conception of the novel, never lost sight of his desire to place his writing in the service of his nation, never wavered from the compelling preoccupation with depicting the Mexican reality. As a consequence, Azuela carried on throughout his life a running battle with professional critics and *literatos*. To the end of his life, Azuela's resistance to the modern was impassioned and stubborn. The distress and anguish which all this caused him can stand reiteration for one paramount reason: Azuela's anguish provides an unmistakable and significant measure of the imbalance that he felt between the pulse of the times and his own pulse. This imbalance is underlined by Azuela's conception of the novel.

Because of his own conception of the novel, first of all, Azuela himself has played no small role in establishing the standards, criteria, and principles by which he has for all practical purposes asked his works be judged, at the expense of their artistic merits. His literary principles and his inability to recognize the merits of the three modern works, must account to some extent for their neglect up to now, and for the incomplete critical estimate which has settled upon Azuela as a novelist. Azuela critics must now face the fact that their benevolent attitude towards Azuela's own conception of the novel has limited the critical estimate of his works.

Azuela's conception and practice of the novel were shaped and influenced by his specific place in time, of which he had an unshakable sense. It is significant that Azuela himself provides the best running commentary of his sense and of his time as he saw it. Several non-fictional works in his *Obras completas* stress the importance of the historical context for Azuela.[4]

Throughout these works Azuela repeatedly emphasized that the first mission of a Mexican novelist was to write a good *Mexican* novel and not a successful literary work (III, 633). He was opposed to the comparison of Mexican and European novelists because he felt such comparisons were demeaning to the Mexicans (III, 624-25). And yet he repeatedly isolated those qualities and traits in the writers about whom he wrote which coincided with the realistic and naturalistic principles of Balzac and Zola. Even the novels of the Mexican Revolution, indeed especially these, which Azuela and his critics have judged to be absent of identifiable foreign influences, are heavily indebted to these two French writers in principle and in spirit. That indebtedness was partly demonstrated in the chapter on *La malhora* of this investigation. More can be said of Balzac's and Zola's influence on Azuela's practice and theories.

A novel, Azuela said, thinking of Balzac, must be a faithful, documented depiction of the life of a nation and of its people. It must contain scenes of real life, must strive after truth even though it be painful and sordid. A good novel is one which is written in the simple, everyday language of the people. In a single expression uttered by a campesino, Azuela insisted, the soul of our people can be compressed (III, 596). A novel must be written, preferably by a man of the people himself, for the masses at large and not for a select audience of specialized readers, other writers and critics. Of professional novelists or *literatos,* Azuela said:

> A literato only needs a few scraps of blank paper to write a book; one who is not [a *literato*] must be propelled to write when he has something to say (III, 1263).

During times of national agony the novelist must give his cry of outrage, "to rend our ears with his cry swelling with all the anguish, the longings and the joys of our people." A novelist must name and indict the social ills which afflict his nation and his people. It is the duty of a novelist, he insisted, to deal with all aspects of society, with all the people, with their lives, their heartaches, sufferings and joys, and with the collective character of his time and his age (III, 1263-65). Because for Azuela, the novelist sums up a culture, a nation and an age (III, 1267).

In these pronouncements, some of them gleaned from writings that date back to 1919, it is now possible to see that Azuela was formulating *ex post facto* the principles and attitudes which had informed his novels of the Mexican Revolution, by then behind him.[5] In the early nonfictional writings as well as in the later ones can be felt the anguish of a man who had lived through a painful social upheaval of which he was its eminent painter and who was witnessing the arrival of a new spirit and a new sensibility in the arts before his own creative work was even recognized. Frequently his criticism, which is valuable because it is that of a practitioner, suffers from excessive sarcasm and vituperation. Azuela's standards and principles, pronounced and proclaimed at every opportunity the rest of his life, echo many statements and declarations of the two French writers for whom he felt the greatest affinity, Balzac and Zola.

For the grand old man of Mexican letters, as late as 1950, Balzac was still the "greatest novelist of all times" (III, 812). And Azuela's estimate of Balzac is based on his having raised the novel, as a faithful, documented representation of the life of the people to the category of great art (Ibid). Azuela repeatedly praised Balzac for being a man of the people, and for the appeal of his works to the common reader, as Azuela considered himself, "setting aside those merits which a critic or a scholar observes and comments" (III, 815). Azuela also admired Balzac's monumental disdain for critics and for "literature." For Azuela, following Balzac, *literature* did not exist; the only thing which exists is life, of which politics and art are only parts. Azuela frequently underlined that both Balzac and Zola were undeservedly neglected or misunderstood for many years and that they were exasperated by the critics (III, 820-33, 921-33).

As a physician, also, Azuela appreciated Zola's objectivity and clinical attention to detail. "Zola's works are as chaste as any treatise on medicine," he said (III, 911). In his discussion of Zola's *L'Assommoir*, Azuela identifies many traits such as characterize his own work, *La malhora* (III, 906-07).

In both Balzac and Zola, in their lives and in their works, then, Azuela found considerable comfort for his own anguish and distress about the critical neglect of his works. Of Balzac's biographer, Stefan Zweig, Azuela asked: "How could he have penetrated the man who suffers all the calamities, the anguish, whose struggle is split against destiny and against himself, with only the belief in his own genius to guide him?" (III, 828). Surely, Azuela had himself in mind too. Given the nature of Azuela's principles and standards, it is no wonder that he abandoned the modern novel. As Azuela saw it, his mission in life was not to make literature but to write about his nation. For this reason naturalism was his life-long mainstay.

In his speech of acceptance of the National Prize in Arts and Sciences, awarded him two years before his death on 26 January 1950 (III, 1286-88), at the age of seventy-seven Azuela declared:

> In truth I would never have written a single line of literature if from my youth the desire to write about our nation had not commanded me with irresistible force, something that was always in bad taste to write about, particularly in those times during which everything, including literature, was being imported from Europe.

This desire made Azuela the creator of the Novel of the Mexican Revolution. In this he is a product of his time; as observer, commentator, and participant Azuela was outraged by the events of the Mexican Revolution. Indeed, his outrage and indignation over the betrayal of the ideals of the Mexican Revolution characterize his novels of the Mexican Revolution and the modern novels as well. "As an independent writer, my norm has always been truth," he says, and his intention was "to render with the greatest fidelity possible a faithful image of our people. . . . To discover and identify our shortcomings has been my goal as a novelist." Like Goya in his times, like Orozco his contemporary, Azuela identified those elements in society which he could condemn: man's inhumanity to man, man's victimization of man.

Azuela recognized in that same speech of acceptance, that the novel of ideas may be encumbered as a work of art,

> but many times I was compelled to say, to cry out what I thought and felt, and not to have done so would have been to betray myself. Not everyone comprehended my attitude and often I was censured for it.

To cry out what he thought and felt, Azuela was led to the discovery of what may be one of his most memorable and significant creations: the character, in several novels, who is his ideological spokesman for the ideals of the Mexican Revolution. Luis Leal, in the conclusion of his admirable work on Azuela, suggests persuasively that Azuela proceeded in a manner not unlike that of the doctor in his clinic.[6] Leal sees a very close connection between Azuela the doctor and Azuela the novelist, between Azuela of the scalpel and Azuela of the pen. To his analysis of the life of a provincial village, of an individual character, or of the nation as a whole, Leal continues, Azuela brings his medical skills of observation and analysis. Life was his clinic, and, afflicted with the illness of the Mexican Revolution, his nation became his patient. In his novels Azuela analyzes the disease from its first symptoms. He follows the effects of disease on the organism as a whole, and proceeds to an examination of the crisis and the convalescence of his nation. Azuela's novels, like his medical profession, says Leal, have a well defined aim which is never lost from sight: to heal Mexico, to restore health to the nation, his own, the source of so much suffering for Azuela.

In the speech of acceptance mentioned above, Azuela confirms that aim:

> If within my possibilities I was able to contribute to
> the work of national affirmation to which reference
> has been made by the Director of the Instituto Na-
> cional de Bellas Artes, the greatest desire of my life
> as a writer shall have been realized.

In the sense that Azuela desired it he did fulfill his greatest desire
as a writer.

Azuela, however, went beyond his own expectations. It was
mentioned at the beginning of this investigation that Azuela's
present international reputation is based on his novels of the
Mexican Revolution. The critical estimate of Azuela which has
dominated Azuela criticism until now was admirably summed up
by John E. Englekirk in 1952, the year of Azuela's death. Englekirk
says:

> Whatever the estimate posterity finally bestow [sic]
> upon Azuela . . . this much at least may be said with
> reasonable certainty now: Mariano Azuela alone
> merits recognition as "*the* novelist of the Mexican
> Revolution."[7]

This estimate of Azuela is unchallengeable. It seems unfair to the
grand old man of Mexican letters, however, that this critical estimate of Azuela as a novelist should be associated generally with
a single work. As Englekirk points out:

> There is little likelihood at this late date of 1952 that
> *Los de abajo* may yet be displaced as *the* novel of the
> Revolution or that anyone may yet produce a body of
> writing on the totality of the Revolution to chal-
> lenge Azuela's right to the distinction of being the
> only novelist to have documented its nearly every
> phase.[8]

Azuela critics in general recognize the importance of the whole
period during which Azuela wrote the novels of the Mexican
Revolution. Reflecting a consensus of opinion Englekirk rightly

states that the works of the revolutionary period constitute Azuela's unique contribution to Mexican literature.[9] After discussing a select list of Azuela's works which he feels are most artistically sound, Englekirk cautiously summarizes his evaluation of Azuela's works:

> From this emotional point in time it may not seem unreasonable to venture the opinion that a relatively high percentage of his twenty-three novels . . . may well deserve to be listed among those works of our age that represent an artistic and interpretative achievement of high order. *Los de abajo* alone has won for its author international repute and a permanent berth among the outstanding American novelists of all time; should an unwarranted oblivion settle down over even the small select list herein offered, *Los de abajo* would remain in any case as Azuela's guarantee of a niche in the memory of men.[10]

Englekirk is eminently fair to Azuela in his summing up. He does not fail to take into account the flaws which even Azuela's sympathetic critics recognize in his works, and he challenges, in Azuela's defense, charges levelled by hostile critics against his novels. The views and critical opinions which Englekirk sums up reflect principles, standards and criteria of no small import. They respect, too much I fear, those of Azuela himself. Unfortunately, Englekirk gives but one paragraph to Azuela's modern period.

The critics' understandable appreciation of Azuela's deeply emotional preoccupation with the life of his nation, the overwhelming import of his works dealing with the Mexican Revolution, and the great sympathy for Azuela's own standards and principles account for the incomplete critical estimate of Azuela today. In his own right Azuela is *the* novelist of the Mexican Revolution! To fulfill his greatest desire as a writer, wishing to avoid blameable concessions that would betray his conception of the novel, Azuela never abandoned his preoccupation with Mexico's identity, nor his life-long adherence to the principles of naturalism. The just appraisal of the documentary quality of Azuela's works, in which historical, social and psychological values are in fact dominant, has resulted to date in an inadequate consideration of Azuela's art in general.

La malhora, El desquite and *La luciérnaga,* this investigation hopes to have demonstrated, invite a balanced re-appraisal of Azuela's art. These three modern works exhibit Azuela's persistent preoccupation with surroundings and social themes: the slums of Mexico City, the sordid life of the modern metropolis; violence, prostitution, alcoholism and degeneracy. This concern with the life of his nation, with its social ills and conditions, makes Azuela a socially conscious precursor of Agustín Yañez, Juan Rulfo and Carlos Fuentes. This fact has been amply recognized.

But Azuela as an artist gave added dimensions to the novel, against his own predilections if you will, without losing his historical and social sense. His three modern novels, consequently, call for a fair re-appraisal of Azuela's artistic achievement, a re-appraisal that will recognize his larger achievement as a novelist. Such a re-appraisal of his art need not minimize the importance of Azuela's having expressed the general state of mind into which he was born and in which he could not help but participate. Because of his personal temperament and because of his definite place in time he could not diminish his greatest desire as a writer: to depict the great social upheaval of his time, the Mexican Revolution. Once this desire was realized, a relative health having settled upon his nation, Azuela felt again compelled to participate in another revolution of this time: an artistic revolution that transformed the esthetic sensibility of the whole twentieth century. Winds of change in the first quarter of the twentieth century swept into Mexico from Europe and North America. The artistic sensibility of the age was energized and raised to new spiritual and intellectual heights. Azuela rose to the height of his times and wrote *La malhora, El desquite* and *La luciérnaga.* The force of the modern spirit was no less compelling than that of the Mexican Revolution. Azuela did not succumb to either; he rose to both occasions!

The artistic principles and qualities of the three modern novels, discussed in this investigation and summarized at the beginning of this concluding chapter, force upon us the fact, as I have stated, that Azuela is the first modern Mexican novelist of the twentieth century. *La malhora, El desquite* and *La luciérnaga* attest to the very close connection which existed in the first quarter of this century between Mexican, European and North American arts and letters. With these modern works Azuela brought the modern Mexican novel into the international mainstream.

By virtue of their combination of naturalism and modernism, the modern works assign to Azuela in the development of the early modern novel in Mexico a role comparable to that of Henry James in the development of the European novel. Azuela turned the novel inward and established himself as the originator of the Mexican novel of consciousness.

Azuela, therefore, is the artistic precursor of Yañez, Rulfo and Fuentes. This fact has not been sufficiently recognized. His modern novels, collectively and in their evolution, pave the way for Yañez's penetrating psychological analysis of character in *At the Edge of the Storm* (1947); for Rulfo's hallucinatory visions "through the window of the grave" in *Pedro Paramo* (1955); and for Fuentes' powerful and painful images of Mexican life and of Mexico City, in such novels as *The Death of Artemio Cruz* (1962) and *Change of Skin* (1965). *La luciérnaga,* then, becomes the first Mexican "landmark novel"[11] of the twentieth century. Azuela, unfortunately, never realized the importance of his having turned the novel inward.

Finally, I suggest that artistic forms also have the added value of serving as barometers of the age and of the artistic sensibility. In the combination of naturalism and modernism of *La malhora, El desquite* and *La luciérnaga,* and in Azuela's conception of the novel, I see a powerful and dramatic conflict between the social commentator and the artist. Azuela was torn between his predilections for traditional forms and principles of the novel and the powerful literary currents rising to the height of the times. Azuela was a man, a writer, split between his desire to document the collective character of his age for the people and the demands of the time to produce more complex and innovative, experimental works of art, between the old and the new. It is necessary, I think, to take this conflict into account to better appreciate his modern novels, to be more sympathetic to their inevitable flaws.

Azuela's resistance to the modern, his running battle with the critics and literati, his distress over his anonymity, were poignant and anguished. In addition to their merits as works of art, the modern novels are documents of one man's inward struggle with himself and his times. Considered in this light, Azuela becomes a barometer of the times and in his own experience there is a kind of recapitulation of the modern spirit's struggle and triumph. An expression of José Ortega y Gasset comes to mind: "Yo soy yo y mi circunstancia;" Azuela did indeed have a keen sense of his own place in time. With *La malhora, El desquite* and *La luciérnaga* Azuela arrived at an artistic plenitude that placed him at the height of the times.

Notes

[1]*Mariano Azuela* (New York: Twayne Publishers, 1971), p. 5.

[2]Prólogo de Francisco Monterde y Bibliografía de Alí Chumacero (México: Fondo de Cultura Económica, vols. I-II, 1958; vol. III, 1960). All subsequent references to *Obras completas* will be indicated by the volume and page numbers and will be included in the text of this study. All translations from Spanish in this study are mine unless otherwise indicated.

[3]See John E. Englekirk, "The Discovery of *Los de abajo*," *Hispania,* XVIII (1935), 53-62.

[4]The definitive critical work on Azuela's life and works at present is Luis Leal's *Mariano Azuela: vida y obra* (México: Ediciones de Andrea, 1961). It contains a very extensive bibliography. For a summary of the main values of the novel of the Mexican Revolution, see F. Rand Morton's *Los novelistas de la Revolución Mexicana* (México: Editorial Cultura, 1949), 241-58.

[5]"La etapa de hermetismo, en la obra del Dr. Mariano Azuela," *Cuadernos Americanos,* II (1952), p. 287.

[6]*Mariano Azuela: vida y obra.* Stated in the Nota Preliminar.

[7]John S. Brushwood and José Rojas Garcidueñas, *Breve historia de la novela mexicana* (México: Ediciones de Andrea, 1959), p. 93.

[8]*Tres novelas de Mariano Azuela* (México: Fondo de Cultura Económica, 1968), p. 11.

[9]In using these terms I am following René Wellek and Austin Warren, *Theory of Literature,* 3rd ed. (1942; rpt. New York: Harcourt, Brace and World, 1956). I do not consider at all tenable, however, their notion that extrinsic factors—for example, biography, society, psychology, history and so on—have nothing to do with literary criticism, interpretation and evaluation.

[10]I am following the 34th ed. (1926; rpt. Madrid: Revista de Occidente, 1960). An English translation is available: *The Revolt of the Masses,* trans. anon. (New York: W. W. Norton, 1957).

[11]Ibid., p. 70.

¹²Ibid. Footnote on p. 74.

¹³For some idea of the present critical debate concerning whether or not Modernism is dead, for example, see Maurice Beebe, "What Modernism Was," *Journal of Modern Literature*, III (1974), pp. 1065-1084. A generous selected bibliography conveys a good sense of the liveliness of the debate.

¹⁴These terms were coined by Wayne C. Booth. The "narrator-agent," as defined by Booth, is an *active* "dramatized narrator." In other words the "narrator-agent" participates in and produces "some measurable effect on the course of events." See *The Rhetoric of Fiction*, 10th ed. (1961; rpt. Chicago: Univ. of Chicago Press, 1970), pp. 151-54. For a summarized discussion of Booth's terms, see Jacques Souvage, *An Introduction to the Study of the Novel*, (Gent: E. Story-Scientia, 1965), pp. 58-60.

¹⁵This view is set forth by numerous critics of Mexican letters. Among them are: Luis Leal, "La nueva narrativa mexicana," *Nueva Novela Hispanoamericana*, II (1972), p. 89; María del Carmen Millan, "Las novelas clásicas de los últimos veinticinco años," *Revista Iberoamericana*, XXXV (1969), p. 525; and Joseph Sommers, *After the Storm: Landmarks of the Modern Mexican Novel* (Albuquerque: Univ. of New Mexico Press, 1968), p. 54.

CHAPTER II

¹These developments and international literary relations are treated in some detail, in Eliud Martínez, "Mariano Azuela and 'The Height of the Times:' A Study of *La luciérnaga*," *Latin American Literary Review*, 3 (1974), pp. 113-130. The discovery of *The Underdogs* is taken up in Chapter III.

²Quotation in English, in Leal, op, cit. (Twayne), pp. 116-17.

³Leal, *Mariano Azuela: vida y obra*, p. 54.

⁴Quoted in *Paths to the Present*, ed. Eugene Weber (New York and Toronto: Dodd, Mead and Co., 1970), p. 143.

⁵Ibid., p. 144.

⁶*Mariano Azuela: vida y obra*, p. 127

⁷Arnold Hauser makes a very good case for the modernism of Stendhal, Balzac, Flaubert and Zola. See *The Social History of Art*

(New York: Vintage-Knopf, 1958), vol. 4, esp. pp. 26-30.

[8]Jacques Souvage explains and discusses the "dramatized novel," in *An Introduction to The Study of the Novel*, pp. 41-60.

[9]Mariano Azuela, *Two Novels of Mexico: The Flies and The Bosses*, trans. Lesley Byrd Simpson (Berkeley and Los Angeles: Univ. of California Press, 1965), p. 19.

[10]Ibid. pp. 19-20, my emphasis.

[11]Ibid., p. 21.

[12]*Mariano Azuela: vida y obra*, p. 54.

[13]*Estridentismo* refers to the first avant-garde school of poetry in Mexico in the twentieth century. In subject matter, forms and techniques it is much indebted to such European tendencies as dada, futurism, imagism and surrealism. See John S. Brushwood, *Mexico in its Novel* (Austin: Univ. of Texas Press, 1966), pp. 189-200; Luis Leal, *Panorama de la literatura mexicana actual* (Washington D. C.: Unión Panamericana, 1968), pp. 37-44; German List Arzubide, *El movimiento estridentista* (Jalapa, Veracruz: Ediciones de Horizonte, n.d.); and Frederick S. Stimson, *The New Schools of Spanish American Poetry* (Madrid: Editorial Castalia, 1970), pp. 132-37.

[14]"La etapa de hermetismo, en la obra del Dr. Mariano Azuela," p. 257.

[15]Preface to *Tres novelas de Mariano Azuela*, p. 13.

[16]The use of this leitmotif in *La luciérnaga* has been studied by Kurt L. Levy, "*La luciérnaga*: Title, Leitmotif, and Structural Unity," *Philological Quarterly*, 51 (1972), pp. 321-28; and Eliud Martínez, "La visión alcohólica de Dionisio en *La luciérnaga* de Mariano Azuela," *Revista Universidad de Sonora*, III (1972), pp. 14-20.

[17]Francisco Monterde, op, cit.

[18]Robert Humphrey, *Stream of Consciousness in the Modern Novel* (Berkeley: Univ. of California Press, 1962), pp. 24, 35 and 127.

[19]The ambiguous ending of *La malhora* had puzzled critics until Azuela resolved the problem. See Bernard M. Dulsey, "Azuela Revisited," *Hispania*, XXV (1951), pp. 331-32.

[20]*Tres Novelas de Mariano Azuela*, p. 13.

CHAPTER III

[1]"The Discovery of *Los de abajo*," pp. 59-60.

[2]*Trayectoria de la novela en México* (México: Ediciones Botas, 1951), p. 167.

[3]Ibid., p. 168.

[4]*Mariano Azuela*, in English (Twayne), p. 68.

[5]Ibid.

[6]Ibid, p. 69.

[7]*Historia de la novela hispanoamericana* (México: Ediciones de Andrea, 1966), pp. 146-49.

[8]*The Mexican Novel Comes of Age* (Notre Dame and London: Univ. of Notre Dame Press, 1971), p. 28.

[9]*Mariano Azuela: vida y obra*, p. 56.

[10]Wayne C. Booth, *The Rhetoric of Fiction*, pp. 151-54; Jacques Souvage, *Introduction to the Study of the Novel*, pp. 58-60. See note 14 of Chapter I.

[11]The discussion of point of view in this chapter is based to a large extent on Norman Friedman's "Point of View in Fiction: The Development of a Critical Concept," *PMLA*, LXX (1955), pp. 1160-84; and on Souvage's survey view of its use in practice and theory, op. cit., pp. 50-60.

[12]*Mariano Azuela: vida y obra*, p. 110.

[13]Robert Humphrey, op. cit., pp. 33-34, 127.

[1]"Towards a Prototype of Mariano Azuela's *La luciérnaga*," *Romance Notes*, 11 (1970), p. 519.

[2]Ibid., p. 521.

[3]Preface to *Tres novelas de Mariano Azuela*, p. 11.

[4]See the chapter, "Griffith and Eisenstein: The Uses of Literature in Film," in Robert Richardson, *Literature and Film* (Bloomington: Indiana Univ. Press, 1972), pp. 44-56.

[5]*Mariano Azuela* (Twayne), p. 71.

[6]*Tres novelas de Mariano Azuela*, p. 16.

[7]Langford, op. cit., p. 28; and Leal, *Mariano Azuela: vida y obra*, p. 61.

CHAPTER V

[1] Norman Friedman, "Point of View in Fiction," p. 1169.

[2] See Azuela's "Mi experiencia en el cine" ("My Experience in Film"), *O. C.* III, 1148-73.

[3] For an excellent brief discussion of montage, see Gerald Mast, *A Short History of the Movies* (New York: Bobbs Merrill, 1971), pp. 192-195.

[4] Among them are the two large autobiographical works, *El novelista y su ambiente*, I and II. Others are *Grandes novelistas, Cien años de novela mexicana* (One Hundred Years of the Mexican Novel), and *Divagaciones literarias (Literary Essays)*. All these works are in vol. III of *O. C.*

[5] Azuela spelled out his credo as a novelist as early as 1919, one year after the last novels of the Mexican Revolution, and four years before he wrote *La malhora* (III, 1263-65).

[6] The following statements paraphrase Leal's comments in *Mariana Azuela: vida y obra*, pp. 132-34. For a more extensive commentary, see Leal, "Mariano Azuela, novelista médico," *Revista Hispánica Moderna*, XXVIII (1962), pp. 295-303.

[7] "Mariano Azuela: A Summing Up (1873-1952)," *South Atlantic Studies for Sturgis E. Leavitt* (Washington D. C.: The Scarecrow Press, 1953), p. 127.

[8] Ibid., p. 129.

[9] Ibid., p. 133.

[10] Ibid., p. 135.

[11] The term is used by Joseph Sommers in *After the Storm: Landmarks of the Modern Mexican Novel*, "in the sense that each work represents a significant new advance in literary expression." p. x.